A Country Boy's Will to Survive

CHRIS BENEAR'S JOURNEY

A TRUE STORY

by

Mary Benear

ISBN: 978-0-578-85937-8 Paperback

Printed in the United States of America.

Library of Congress Control Number: 2021905195

Any errors in references to events, historical events, places, people, and names are unintentional.

Cover designs by Alex Reis and Janet Weber
Interior book design by Janet Weber
Cover photo by Nathan Findlay

First printing edition 2021

Publisher - Mary Benear
Howell, MI 48855
marybenear@gmail.com

(signature)

To my son, Chris Benear, for his desire,

determination, and will to survive.

Lynnie

Thanks for your Support.

Take the Time to count your
Blessings!

Team Benear
Mary

Preface

This is a Mother's story of her son's will to survive: His determination, courage and struggle to survive a horrible accident, and his internal drive to get back to the life he once enjoyed.

It is a story of her husband's special bond between himself and his son. Of a Dad's courage and fight to make sure everything was being done for his buddy.

It is a story of two special daughters and their extraordinary, unwavering, and endless devotion and love for their little brother and their parents.

It is a story of family members coming together to keep us going through such an excruciating time in our life.

It is a story of many friends who stepped up and went above and beyond to help our family get through the trying times we found ourselves in.

It is a story of doctors, nurses, first responders, and police officers who helped our son.

I've heard that some people who have written books come down with writer's block. In my case I would have memory blocks on a few events. So I would sit down with some of the friends and family who helped us through those events when they were happening and we would reminisce. The details would become clearer after a short refresh of my memory and then the writing came a little easier.

Our son, Chris, was born on July 25, 1983. He was such a cute kid (No bias on my part.☺). He was even named the Howell Melon Prince, for the annual Howell Melon Festival, at the age of two. He was an outdoor kid from the start. He loved hunting, fishing, and riding and working on motorcycles with his dad. He played travel baseball, lots of basketball, but I think football was his love. High school came and it was going to be Chris' time to shine. Sadly he suffered a torn meniscus, a broken tibia which required a rod and plates with follow up surgery to remove some screws and a plate from the rod, and then a torn anterior cruciate ligament dashed his dreams completely. His high school career was over. Chris really never had his chance to shine. After high school, Chris played on adult softball teams, and hunting was still his love. He has always lived in Howell, Michigan near his childhood home which kept him close to the family farm and lots of aunts, uncles, and cousins that live in the area.

The tears flowed easily as we would talk about the different post-accident stages Chris and our family went through, but in a lot of ways it was healing. When you are going through life changing events, you don't have time to think about the magnitude of what your loved one, your family, or you are going through.

Every day brought a new set of challenges and emotions. You are busy just living the life you have been dealt at that time and making the best of it.

MY NEW GUIDELINE

God doesn't give us what we can handle,

God helps us handle what we are given.

– Anonymous

Chapter 1 – A Good Day

Sunday

June 5, 2011

It was a gorgeous Sunday morning so my husband Jeff and I set out for Byron Center, just outside of Grand Rapids, Michigan, for our grandson Jack's third birthday party. We had no idea that later that day our son Chris' life was to be in danger and that all of our lives were about to change in ways we couldn't have imagined.

Chris had been over to our house late Saturday afternoon. He lived around the corner from us about half a mile away. He was going to mow our lawn, but he had told his dad that he was a little tired and hot and asked him if he would mind mowing. Jeff had readily agreed.

Chris had always wanted to mow our lawn because he took pride in how great his mow lines looked. My mow lines looked a little crooked, like I had been drinking, so I was not asked to mow anymore. Dad had a much straighter eye, so as Dad mowed, Chris went inside to cool off in the air conditioning and have some iced tea.

I arrived home Saturday afternoon from our daughter Stephanie's bridal shower which was held at her friend Heather's house just south of town about twelve miles away. Jeff was mowing. He smiled and waved as I drove by. After I had entered the house I found Chris watching television and relaxing.

"Hi Chris, how's it going? Dad's mowing?"

"Yeah! I just did three lawns and I needed a break. I'm tired and it's pretty warm," said Chris.

"That's fine. He looks like he's enjoying it. Mow lines look good." We both laughed.

Chris was extremely busy that spring and summer. He had been working as an electrician's apprentice with just one test left to take to get his electrician's license. He was laid off from his regular electrician's team so he had hired on with another company and a couple of builders to finish accruing hours toward his license. He was also running his lawn mowing business, CB Lawn Services now called Benear's Outdoor Services, which he had started while still in high school. At that time, he was mowing around seventeen to twenty lawns a week with a few lawns scheduled every other week. Chris was an extremely hard worker. He was finally seeing some of his hard work pay off with the purchase of a house in 2009 at the age of twenty-six. His goal was to have it paid off by the time his dad reached the age of 65 and was able to retire in 2020. Chris figured they could go on a lot of hunting trips and motorcycle adventures together if his bills were small. He never passed up a job to make an extra buck, but he tried to take Sundays off.

As Chris' friends could tell you, Chris had three priorities: number one – his dad, number two – hunting, and number three – his family. He also found time to play in a softball league a couple of nights a week, did some fishing, went on bike rides, and enjoyed an occasional date. When fall arrived, things slowed down because of hunting season. He hunted whitetail deer which took priority over almost everything. Hunting with a bow and arrow was more challenging than a gun and Chris loved the challenge. Chris spent a lot of time in the woods scouting and preparing his blinds to help ensure a successful hunting season.

It was unusual for him to ask his dad to mow or for him to take a break from his busy schedule. While he cooled off inside, I refilled Chris' tea. As I handed the tea to him, he said, "Mom, I'm not riding with you and Dad to Jack's party tomorrow." Jack is our daughter Amanda's son. "Why?" I had asked. "I'm just behind on my lawns and I need to do four lawns tomorrow morning. Tonight I still need to go to Heather's and take down the tent from Stephanie's party. So I told Amanda that I would drive up after I'm done with my lawns," Chris responded. "Okay, just don't overdo it tomorrow. It's supposed to be really hot," I said. The weather forecaster was calling for a high of 95 degrees and sunny.

We arrived at a park in Byron Center around noon that Sunday for the birthday party and it was already getting warm. Amanda had planned to hold Jack's party at a local little kids' ball field. Amanda always does such a good job planning her parties. For Jack's birthday, each child received a bat and ball as their party favor. We loved watching the moms and dads running around with their children chasing balls. It brought back some good memories of my three kids and all their cousins' countless hours in their grandma's front yard playing kickball and other games. Jack and his friends stopped long enough to eat watermelon, ice cream, and cake. It had been a good day! No one was ready to leave the party, but it was half past two in the afternoon and Chris had not made it there yet.

Around three o'clock Chris called and informed me that he had decided not to make the ninety minute drive to the party. He had just finished lawns for the day and needed to be home by 7:00 p.m. to take delivery of a motorcycle he was going to purchase. He hadn't felt he had time to get to the party and back by 7:00 p.m., but he did have time to go to a nearby lake and swim with some buddies. He could easily make it home from there by 7:00 p.m. He asked me to tell Amanda not to be mad and that he would make it up to Jack later. I told him they would be bummed, but I understood that it was a long drive. I told Chris that Dad and I would stop at his house on our way home to see his new bike, and that we would probably get there around 7:30 p.m. He said, "Great, I'll be there." We left the party and went back to Amanda's house for a while before heading home.

Around 7:30 p.m. Sunday evening we were almost home. We had tried calling Chris, but it went straight to his voice mail. We hadn't thought too much about it, he could have been talking to the guy selling him the bike or out for a joyride on his new bike. We had reached Chris' road, so we headed to his house to see the new bike. Chris and his dad loved riding motorcycles, but they were usually dirt bikes. The Harley would be Chris' first road bike. Chris still wasn't home.

No bike. No truck. No Chris. We tried calling again while we were still at his house, and again it went right to his voice mail. We headed home continuing to call off and on for the next few hours. Jeff finally drove the four-wheeler over to his house around 9:30 p.m., still no Chris. Chris was twenty-seven so he didn't have to let us know where he was all the time, but he knew we had planned to stop at his place to see his 'new' motorcycle. Chris not being there when he said he would be was very unusual. He was really good about letting us know if plans had changed.

We went to bed around 10:00 p.m. thinking it was strange that we hadn't heard from Chris after all of the messages we had left on his cell phone. This was not like Chris at all.

Chapter 2 – Nightmare News

Monday – Day 1

June 6, 2011

Jeff's alarm was due to go off around 5:00 a.m., but it never had a chance. Around 4:45 a.m. the doorbell rang which startled both of us. I said, "Jeff, it's for you!" The last time our doorbell rang in the middle of the night, I was home alone. I had thought someone was trying to break in around half past two in the early morning hours. It had ended up being a young man high on something mistakenly thinking he was home and just forgot his keys. After I had made a 911 call, the responders found the guy throwing up in my husband's car which he had thought was his own. The officer had called for an ambulance when they realized the kid was medically in trouble. That had all been very unsettling. I was just as unsettled this time, even with Jeff home.

The doorbell rang again. As Jeff was trying to get his bearings, I beat him out of bed. I headed down the hallway toward the front door. As I reached the end of the hallway with Jeff right behind me, we heard the doorbell ring again and a man yelling, "This is the police." We saw flashlights coming through our front window and my heart sank. "This can't be good," I said to Jeff as I opened the front door to two police officers. One of them stated, "We are looking for Jeff Benear." I asked if it was Chris as Jeff answered, "I'm him." The officer asked if Jeff owned a green Dodge pickup. We both looked at each other and we knew something had happened to Chris and it had to be BAD. Jeff had answered yes to the officer's question and said, "My son is driving it." The officer stated that there had been an accident and that they were transporting Chris to the University of Michigan (U of M) hospital in Ann Arbor. We both stood there in shock!

The officer then told us that my sister Carol had come with them to show the officers which house was ours so they could get to us a little faster. As we saw Carol approach the front door we didn't understand how she was involved. Carol gave me a hug and said, "I'm so sorry Mary. I just didn't recognize who it was." Still not understanding, I said, "What?" She said, "He was so covered with mud and dirt that he was unrecognizable to me. I'm so sorry." "What do you mean you didn't know it was Chris, he's your nephew?" Was Chris not able to speak when she saw him? How could Carol not know him! Chris had just wired the new addition to their house. She saw him regularly. Carol had nothing more to say. We hurriedly dressed, and grabbed my purse, keys, and phones. Carol had made us a drink to take with us. We headed for the car.

The shortest auto route to Ann Arbor was down Allen Road to Latson Road which took us right by the scene of the accident. Carol had said that they found his car in a ravine right down the road from her house. As we approached the scene, it was easy to see the flashing lights in the dark of the early morning hours. It had looked like there were around four police cars and a fire truck parked by the edge of the road. The sleepy tree lined country road was eerily lit and unnervingly awake for this early morning hour in what would normally have been a dark, quiet, peaceful country setting.

We pulled further up the road to drop Carol off at her place and saw that her husband Robert was standing at the edge of their driveway. Jeff's window went down and he asked, "What can you tell us Rob? Do you know what happened? How bad is Chris?" Finally Robert had a chance to answer, "I don't know Jeff. I just don't know." He stood there shaking his head. We could see with all of the flashing lights and the side yard light that Robert looked as white as a ghost. We could tell by his eyes and how he hung his head that it wasn't good.

We made very few phone calls on our thirty-five minute drive to the hospital in Ann Arbor. I called our daughters, Chris' sisters Amanda and Stephanie, and my sister Betty. All I could tell them was that they were transporting Chris to the U of M hospital in Ann Arbor by ambulance, that he had been in an accident, and that it looked like just his vehicle was involved. We decided not to tell them that Robert and Carol didn't even recognize him. They all had a long drive ahead of them. Stephanie later told me that I called her three times not making much sense during any of the calls. She did understand that Chris was at U of M hospital, and that he had been in an accident. Jeff called his work and I called my work. I do remember me telling Jeff to slow down about three times. I did a lot of praying. Jeff and I hardly spoke the rest of the way to the hospital. Our thoughts were flying in so many different directions.

We had questions and we needed answers. How bad could it be if his Aunt and Uncle didn't recognize him? If Carol and Rob would have recognized him we could have been by Chris' side sooner. I was angry that it took so long. Why and how did the truck end up at the bottom of the ravine? It must have been thirty feet down to the bottom, and it was usually wet.

We finally entered the emergency department entrance parking lot. Jeff had barely stopped the car when we both jumped out. Thank goodness as we entered the door a young man working as the emergency entrance valet asked us our name. Jeff threw him the keys so that he could park our car.

Upon entering the outer emergency department doors, we had told them that our son Chris was just brought in by ambulance. A woman said, "Follow me." She escorted us into the emergency department section and headed us toward Chris. It was all a bit surreal. I don't remember whether the emergency department was busy. I don't remember a lot of people running around like you usually picture when you hear 'emergency department'. We followed her to the right where we passed the emergency department station area and passed some curtains. She pointed to the next curtain and stated that Chris was in there.

As we walked toward the curtain, two staff members in scrubs came out of Chris' closed curtain area. I overheard one of them saying to the other, "Another dumb kid not wearing a helmet." If you know me, you would know that I really don't have a problem speaking my mind at certain times, and this was one of those times. "He was in a truck," I yelled, "He was in a truck not on a motorcycle with no helmet!" They said they were sorry and walked away.

Jeff had already walked inside the curtained area so I followed and there lay Chris. He was covered with dried blood, dirt, and gravel. His head was so swollen. He looked so helpless. Jeff was holding his hand. Jeff said, "We're here Chris, its mom and dad. We're here buddy." I approached the other side of the bed, grabbed his hand and said, "Chris, I'm here, its mom."

A staff person was still cleaning around his head trying to remove all the dirt and blood by his eyes and ears. I remember him being especially careful. I was so thankful for the caring way he attended Chris. Suddenly I had to leave. I could feel my legs get a little wobbly and the tears started to really flow. I didn't want to break down in front of Chris so I left the room. I walked out of the room and there were my sister Betty and her husband Dave. Family is everything at times like these. Betty walked with me out of the emergency department for a minute and Dave headed in to be with Jeff.

As Dave and Jeff were in the room, Jeff had his first encounter with the doctor in charge of Chris' case; her name was Dr. Yang. She came in and started to go over Chris' charts. She soon shook her head and murmured as she stared at the computer screen, "This isn't good. I've seen these kinds of wounds before. He will probably never walk or talk again. It's not good. With that said, we never know how it will play out." Jeff's response was, "What do you mean this isn't good. This isn't your average kid. He's really strong!" Jeff had felt so helpless.

Our daughter Stephanie and her fiancé Alex came in shortly after we arrived. As they entered the emergency department, Jeff and I were over to the side talking to one of the doctors who were running tests. As Stephanie and Alex were beside Chris' bedside, Chris grabbed her arm and tried pulling her down toward him. Alex and Stephanie were shocked! They said he mumbled and noises came out, but everything he had tried to say was very incoherent.

Those first hours were so hard on all of us. I thought that everything seemed to be happening so slowly. Doctors came in. Doctors went out. Staff continued to clean Chris off. The wounds on his legs became very visible. They had moved us over to a little private room as they were preparing to move Chris to an intensive care wing. The doctors periodically informed us of new discoveries on his condition as test results came in.

My sister Nancy and her husband Steve were with us as the doctor told us that something had penetrated his skull on the left side, but it seemed to have pulled back out. They were pretty sure nothing was left inside his brain because the X-rays showed no foreign objects. Nothing made sense. We had more questions than ever now.

Why was Chris' right leg covered with a couple of massive wounds that looked like road burns? His right ankle looked huge and was a solid bruise. Why wasn't he coming around? Something went into his skull? Now I realized why the staff thought he was riding a motorcycle without a helmet. Now I understood why Carol and Robert didn't recognize him. Why wasn't staff doing more for him? I really believed they didn't have a lot of hope for his survival. His brain kept swelling. The doctor didn't have anything else to tell us at that point. The doctor had left the consultation room with the rest of us not knowing what, if anything, could be done for Chris. We needed to feel like there was something more that could be done for him. We were *desperate* to hear that something more could be done.

After the doctor left, Jeff threw his glasses across the consultation room. Steve put a strong hand on his shoulder and told Jeff to hang in there. The silence was deafening.

At that point, Amanda had arrived from Grand Rapids. I could hear her breaking down outside of the visitors' waiting room in the hallway. She had arrived and immediately gone in to see Chris not realizing that a consult was happening so no one was in his room with him at that moment. I so wanted one of us to be with her when she first saw her brother. When I raced into the hall my sister Sally was holding her and trying to console her. Amanda turned and saw me. I could see in her eyes how terrified she was. We hugged hard and held hands as we walked into the waiting room. Amanda had realized immediately how it looked so she called her husband Justin to come and be with us.

Our children are very close in age and have always been close as siblings. Amanda was born in 1980, Stephanie in 1982, and Chris in 1983. It was heartbreaking to see Chris lying in that emergency room, and his sisters so concerned and fearful for him. Hugs from the girls had meant so much at that time, it kept Jeff and I going. We wanted Chris to be able to hug us, and for us to be able to hug him too. We needed a miracle.

They moved Chris to the Trauma/Burn Intensive Care unit (T/B ICU) in the late morning that same day. We were allowed two visitors at a time in intensive care so we took turns. Jeff spent most of the time next to Chris as family and friends filed in taking turns.

The T/B ICU had a really large waiting room. As I remember, it was a long and wide room. It had filled up quite quickly with our family and friends. By late afternoon and early evening the room was almost full. 'Team Benear' was pretty impressive. It had been a long day of worry over Chris' chances of survival for all of us. Having so many family and friends there meant so much to Jeff and me. We realized that in that time of tragedy, we were still very blessed.

Making trips back and forth between the waiting room and Chris' room, I learned that they were going to do another MRI and they continued to relieve the pressure off his brain and kept running tests. Finally a report had come in that showed something foreign was still located in his brain near the puncture wound. It was not metal or glass which would be more defined. They thought that it may be wood. No one was sure.

Jeff came back into the waiting room and gathered us all in a big circle. He was holding it together the best he could, trying to speak between his tears and all of his emotions coming to the surface. He told us how bad it looked. He said what a tough kid Chris was, but that Chris and his family needed all the prayers we could get. We needed a miracle for Chris to come back to us. He started praying 'The Lord's Prayer' as we all held hands and joined in.

As soon as the prayer stopped Stephanie broke down and started to collapse. I saw Justin grab her. The emotions of everyone had come to the surface. Jeff went to Stephanie, hugged her, and told her we all needed to be strong for Chris and that Mom and Dad needed her and Amanda to help us get through this for Chris. I felt so helpless and weak at that moment, I just didn't know what to do.

It was in the early morning hours of Tuesday when I had time to realize that we still had no idea exactly what had happened. This added to the uncertainty of what was to come next for Chris and our whole family and it scared me.

Someone brought 'Team Benear' a writing journal on the second day. The journal was for family, friends, and visitors to write Chris a message that he could read when he recovered. What a great idea, and I am very thankful for the journal! Although difficult, each day family and friends would write their thoughts and feelings down in the hopes that it would somehow help Chris, and it seemed to be therapeutic for some of us.

JOURNAL ENTRY – June 6th

1:30 p.m.

Chris came off sedation, and they took him off his pain meds. His vitals were solid. Chris was responding to voices and moving his whole left side (foot, toes, leg, hand, and arm)! He's trying to make contact with us. ☺ Keep praying!

3:30 p.m.

Chris responded to my talking! He grabbed and squeezed Dad's and my hands. He was trying to grab his tube with his left arm and when I wouldn't let him, he moved his right arm! Such success. ☺ He was fighting hard to open his eyes!

♡ Steph

Chapter 3 – Accident Report

Tuesday – Day 2

June 7, 2011

Late in the afternoon our girls had promised they would spend the night with Chris so Dad and I could go home. Chris was unable to communicate verbally so between Jeff, Amanda, Justin, Stephanie, Alex, and me we decided to have at least one of us in the room with Chris 24/7. We had realized early on that this was going to be a long journey, but we were Chris' voice.

We had to learn what he needed and relay his needs to the nurses and doctors. We always tried to have two people spend the night so we could take shifts in his room. At times it was extremely frustrating because we could not always understand what he was asking for and we didn't know what would help him. At other times, we didn't know at all if he even understood what was happening. The communication from Chris in the early days was almost nothing. He uttered a few sounds here and there, but usually with his eyes closed. As his family we had to speak for him.

Alex had offered to drive us home to change clothes, sleep, shower, and pack a few things. We knew we had a long haul in front of us so we decided to take advantage of his offer.

As Alex drove us home, I slept off and on in the back seat while Jeff and Alex kept a conversation going. As we drove by the Salmon house, Robert just happened to be headed out of his driveway. We pulled off to the side of the road and Jeff asked Robert if he had found out anything new. He said that the Livingston County Sheriff's Department had sent out an accident investigator early yesterday morning which would have been June 6. The investigator had spent time recreating what the accident scene and evidence showed. After talking to Robert, Jeff and Alex walked Chris' path and noticed some details. The following account of Chris' accident is taken from the investigator's report, the first responding officers police report, and what Jeff and Alex noticed.

Chris' truck was headed westbound on Allen Road between Latson and Fisher. He had just passed the Salmon family barn which sits on a hill on the south side of Allen Road. As the vehicle approached the top of the hill, it seemed to drift off the road to the south. His vehicle had crossed the center of the roadway onto the grass where it appeared the truck's left tires were in the grass with the right tires seemingly still on the road. His vehicle ran along the fence row approximately one hundred and forty feet hitting some broken and dead branches along the fence which was later found to have green paint on it.

The vehicle had to go up a small embankment to get back up to the dirt road from the grassy side before it reentered the road completely. I can only believe that Chris had passed out, but that his foot must have continued to slightly press on the gas pedal to keep the vehicle rolling, because the vehicle veered back across Allen Road to the north approximately ninety-five yards. The truck then went down a twenty-five foot ravine slope bouncing back and forth hitting trees on the right side and then the left. The vehicle ended up front end first in the water hole at the bottom of the ravine.

A tree limb had penetrated Chris' skull either from the broken and dead branches on the south side or as he veered down the ravine on the North side where his truck hit several trees. No report could say for sure where the head injury actually occurred.

Chris had left his friends at the lake at half past six which would have put him at the accident scene around six forty-five. Based on the accident report, the weather was clear and the roadway appeared to be level with a limited amount of loose gravel and free of major debris that could have contributed to the crash. Speed was not a factor and there seemed to be no evasive driving. The accident report stated that drugs and/or alcohol seemed not to be involved as the cause of the accident.

The report had also stated that Chris was not wearing a seat belt, which really bothered my husband because Chris always wore his seat belt. In fact, Chris would remind us to buckle our seatbelts. The first chance Jeff had, he inspected the seat belt in the truck and there was blood on only one spot on the belt. Jeff had to pull the seatbelt out to see the blood stain. It matched exactly the spot below the head injury if it was being worn. We are convinced that Chris had worn his seat belt. Jeff tried to have the report adjusted, but to no avail.

Chapter 4 – Will to Survive

Monday – Day 1

June 6, 2011

We consider what Chris had accomplished in getting help for himself to save his own life as a MIRACLE. The doctors later told us that this was a true survival story because of his head injury. His brain should not have been able to function well enough for him to take the actions he had to take to survive. His nickname at the hospital became RAMBO.

Chris spent the next NINE hours getting help. We have no idea how long he had been blacked out during his ordeal.

We believed that Chris had somehow released his seat belt and opened his door. The driver's side door handle was broken off on the inside. We don't know when this happened. Did Chris break the handle trying to get out of the car? We knew he had exited his vehicle at the bottom of the ravine and fallen into the swamp water.

Jeff had examined the grass around the west side of the water hole which was on the driver's side of the truck, and he found that it had been really matted down. It had appeared that Chris had spent some time there thrashing around. Chris had dragged himself over to the truck and tried to pull himself up onto the truck. There were muddy palm prints all the way to the top of the truck bed on the rear driver's side. The strength that it took to pull himself up like that, in his condition, was amazing. His path showed that he headed toward the road.

Thank goodness he headed south toward the road! If he would have headed west where there was a closer house would they have been home? Would their door have been unlocked for him to reach them or a phone? Could he have gotten help? Going north would have taken him into thirty-five acres of woods where he probably would have bled to death. The truck was not visible from the road and no one knew there had been an accident. His thought processes must have been working at that point. Thank God he didn't black out in the water hole or he could have drowned.

We still don't know why the accident happened, but thank goodness his survival skills had kicked in.

Chapter 5 – Survival Path

Monday – Day 1

June 6, 2011

Due to his injuries, Chris had to drag himself up the ravine slope because we believe that the right side of his body was paralyzed at that point in time. The limb that penetrated the left side of his skull had affected his ability to move anything on his right side. The slope down to the bottom of the ravine was at a thirty degree incline and he had to drag himself up that incline to get out to the road. The amount of strength it had taken him to do this is still unbelievable to us! Chris is six foot four inches and was around 200 pounds at the time. That is a lot of mass to drag twenty-five feet up at a thirty degree angle! When he reached the road, he headed east toward his Aunt Carol's and Uncle Robert's house.

Chris then dragged himself across the road to the South. He had driven up a hill so we believe he knew that if he had stayed on the

North side of the road a car traveling West coming over the hill might not have seen him in the dark. Chris dragged himself about ninety-eight yards down the road across the street from his Aunt and Uncle's driveway. Chris' drag marks from his six foot four inch, 200 pound frame resembled an inch worm's movements. The distance was almost a football field an inch at a time.

Finally seeing the driveway on the other side of the street, Chris dragged himself back across the road and down the driveway about another forty-two yards to the Salmon's back door. Chris had wired the Salmon's new addition and he knew there was a back door there which they never locked. _Thank you_ for not locking your back door. (They do lock it now, so don't get any ideas. ☺)

Chris had proceeded to get the back door open which was located on the west side of the house. We can't imagine the power it took to reach up high enough to open this door with a paralyzed right side. The back door opened up into a utility room where he then had to maneuver up two steps to the kitchen. They said there was a pool of blood at the top of the second step. That must have been an excruciating obstacle to overcome. Chris managed to push the kitchen table against the windows and knocked over a couple of chairs. No one responded. Everything that was loose ended up on the floor on his way through the kitchen.

After Chris left the kitchen, his path indicated that he had crawled across the living room to the east side of the house. The first room was usually occupied by Chris' twelve year old nephew. He seemed to know he needed to bypass this room. The next room down the hallway was where he knew he would find his Aunt and Uncle. Uncle Robert was startled awake by a light tapping sound on the wall and moaning in the hallway. Before he got out of bed, he reached over to the right and realized Carol was still in bed with him. It couldn't be her in the hallway. Robert exited the bedroom and reached across the hallway to turn on the light. As Robert was looking for the light switch someone grabbed his arm. Robert swatted the hand away yelling, "Who the hell are you?" Robert said that the intruder looked right at him with big white eyes then his body slumped completely to the ground. At the time, Robert felt that the intruder sensed that someone would help him. Robert had been startled awake, but he had finally realized that this person really needed help. He knew this guy wasn't going to harm his family, but were there others?

When Robert had described the intruder, he said he was covered in gravel, wet, and bleeding. At this point, the lights were on and he knew the intruder was hurt badly. As the intruder lay in the middle of his hallway he had no idea who it was or how he had entered their house. Robert yelled to Carol to call 911.

Carol had dialed 911 and grabbed her son out of the first bedroom. Robert had ushered his three girls out the back and sent them all over to Grandma's house with their Uncle Todd who Robert had quickly called to come get the kids. Robert searched the rest of the house and decided this guy was on his own. The 911 call was made at 3:44 on the morning of June 6, 2011.

The first responders were notified that an unknown subject was passed out inside a residence, a possible breaking and entering (B&E)

on Allen Road. The police officers had been told of blood, an intruder, and that the residents of the house had no physical altercations with the intruder. Aunt Carol stated that Robert yelled at the intruder several times before he joined her in the yard, "Who are you? Are you drunk? How did you get here?" I am sure Robert used some more explicit words. There were a few moans then nothing. The police had called for an ambulance while they were on their way to the scene.

When the police arrived on site, they made contact with Robert and Carol in the driveway of their residence. Robert told them that the intruder had entered the house from the west back door. The two officers entered into the residence through the open back door escorted by Robert. They saw a blood trail through the kitchen. They followed the blood trail out of the kitchen, across the living room, and into the hallway where the intruder was lying on his back. They observed that the subject had an open cut on the left side of his head that was bleeding and that he had other cuts and abrasions on his legs, head, and face. He was wet and had dirt and gravel spread throughout his body and face. He was wearing shorts, a t-shirt, and no shoes or sandals. They then advised central dispatch to have the Emergency Medical Service (EMS) run priority due to the intruder's injuries.

Waiting for the ambulance, the officers attempted to speak to the intruder who was currently conscious. They asked him to identify himself, and asked him if he had been in an accident, however, he could not speak to them. He had moved his arms, legs, and head very slowly. He was moaning and appeared to have trouble keeping his eyes open.

Neither officer indicated that they smelled any odor of intoxicants while speaking to the subject. While they were waiting for the EMS to arrive, the intruder had looked like he was going to vomit. The deputy rolled him on his side to prevent him from aspirating. He vomited after he was turned on his side. The EMS team had arrived on the scene, and the officer yelled, "Hurry he's choking on his fluids." They began treating the intruder and transported him immediately to the U of M hospital in Ann Arbor. They had talked of getting a helicopter, but they felt that he had no chance of survival if they waited. The officer looked at Robert as they took the subject out of the residence and said that he didn't think he would ever make it to the U of M hospital alive.

As the ambulance left, the officer asked Robert, "Do you know who the intruder is? Did you see a car or hear anyone just drive away?" "No," was Robert's response. They followed the blood trail and tracks out the back door and to the road. Robert said that he had left his house around six o'clock on the tractor and nothing looked out of place at that time. When he had returned later around 7 o'clock, there was a limb hanging over the edge of the north side of the road just west of his house a ways. He had seen nothing else, especially not a vehicle.

The police told Robert to stay in the driveway as they continued to follow the subject's path. They followed the drag mark trail across the road to the south, down the road to the west, then back across the road to the north. A fire truck had arrived on the scene and everyone had searched the surrounding area with lights and flashlights.

A light had finally illuminated the truck down in the ravine. They yelled back at Robert asking if he knew anyone who drives a green Dodge truck. "Yes, my nephew Chris and a couple of neighbors have green vehicles like that," Robert had replied. Neighbors in a farming community could be within a four to five mile radius. Two officers went down to investigate the vehicle and found a business card with the name Chris Benear on it. They checked the surrounding woods and other areas and determined that there seemed to be no other occupant. They observed a trail from the water hole up the ravine which was consistent with the trail the subject would have had to have crawled.

At this point, Carol and Robert had walked down Allen Road and had seen the vehicle they had found in the ravine. The officers informed them that they had a business card with the name Chris Benear on it from the truck. "That is my nephew!" Carol said. For the first time, Carol and Robert realized the intruder was their nephew Chris.

With all of this information to take in Alex, Jeff, and I headed home. Some things had become clearer and some of our questions were starting to be answered. However, we still didn't know what had caused Chris to black out. Exhaustion had set in after spending close to 37 hours at the hospital, on the drive, and stopping at the accident site. We needed sleep.

Chapter 6 – Sleepless

Tuesday – Day 2

June 7, 2011

Although all of our kids had been out of the house for years, the house had seemed extremely quiet and lonely when we finally arrived home. Jeff and I got busy packing everything we thought we would need for the return trip to the hospital, returned a few phone calls, and went to bed. We were drained, exhaustion had set in. Alex needed to go home, but had promised he would be there when we woke up to head back to the hospital.

Sleep was hard to come by. With everything so quiet I broke down and Jeff tried to console me, but he was struggling with it as much as I was. All night long it seemed as though we were both trying to cope with what had happened to Chris and why. They always say that 'everything happens for a reason,' but we could not come up with any good reason for this to have happened to him. Chris was a very responsible young adult; a homeowner, paid his bills, loved his family and friends, and he tried to do what was right. There were so many unanswered questions.

Then my thoughts had turned to my Mom and how she would react to the news about Chris. Mom had been going through her own battle. She had a major stroke in November of 2010 and needed around the clock assistance. We lost my Dad in June of 1991 so it was up to her ten children to take care of her. Our family was like every other family, siblings and their families move away, and almost everyone was working a full time job.

Mom had paid for a policy for extended care in case something major ever happened to her. When it came time to use the policy, she really just wanted to be at home. The extended care policy covered around five hours of extra care a day. We had them cover the middle of the day and then family members, that were able, took turns rotating in and out to cover the rest of the day. This had been going on for eight months and seemed to be working out. Mom had raised ten children and was a farmer's wife with a heart of gold. She knew the meaning of hard work and the importance of _family_.

She had always made us feel special and made sure that we had everything we needed. Chris and his grandma had a very special relationship. They had enjoyed spending time with each other, especially playing cards together. Chris claimed he was her favorite, but all her grandkids could claim the same; that is just how Grandma made them feel. It would have been extremely hard for me to tell her about Chris' condition. She had already been told he was in an accident, but we were trying not to over worry her. We really hadn't known exactly what to tell her because we hadn't known what was going to happen. I knew it would be very hard seeing her at that point so I let my sisters be her source of information for now.

Sleep had finally come...

Chapter 7 – One Day at a Time

Wednesday – Day 3

June 8, 2011

Alex and Jeff were having a coffee when I had finally woken up. They said they were ready to leave as soon as I could get ready. As I was walking across the family room, a glass jar had fallen out of my hand and shattered all over the place. I knelt down on the floor to pick up the pieces when Alex bent down to help. Alex looked at me and said, "This is probably a bad time to tell you this, but last night during the storm, lightening hit the tree in the front yard. The tree is now covering the driveway so I couldn't drive up to the house."

Really, I hadn't even registered that we had a storm last night. When something this traumatic happens to your family, little things don't seem to be so important. It puts a lot of things into perspective on your priority list.

We would have to deal with the tree later. We walked around the tree to Alex's car and were on our way back to Chris. As we arrived at the hospital, Steph let us know the night went pretty well for Chris. She said that he had moved his right arm. Since he was injured on the left side of his brain, it had affected his right side. Any movement on his right side was great to see. Some of the cousins had taken turns with his sisters in Chris' room during the night. Cousin Liz had been totally startled when Chris moved his left leg bending it at the knee. The swelling in his head and his right leg had gone down considerably. Chris had seemed to be there, but not really there.

They moved Chris up to the Neurological Intensive Care Unit (NICU) on the fourth floor which would become our new home for the next three weeks. Down the hallway was a decent sized waiting room which had become our temporary home. Family and friends had set up a food delivery system so that we always had someone bringing a dinner or homemade goodies. We wanted for nothing more in the munchie department. The room had become well known to the staff that helped out with Chris' treatments as being a friendly place with snacks always available to hold them over. Especially the young interns had seemed to find the time to stop by to say hello. Family and friends had made it so much easier to concentrate on Chris because they were taking care of everything else for us. Blessed!

I had mentioned earlier that family is everything at stressful times in your life. On June eighth, our niece Emily B took it upon herself to find out where they had towed Chris' truck after the accident. She contacted the towing company and set up having the truck towed to

Chris' house. They agreed so she went to meet them and paid the tow bill at Chris' place. She searched the truck and found Chris' cell phone, but no wallet.

Once she brought the phone to the hospital we charged it. Luckily Chris did not have a security lock on it so we were able to listen to his messages. The first return call I made was to the motorcycle owner he was to meet the night of the accident. I explained Chris' situation. He had understood and sent his best wishes. He mentioned that he really liked Chris. He thought he was a really nice kid. The next call was to a company that Chris had recently interviewed with for a new position. They were offering him the job. It was bitter-sweet listening to that message, he had really wanted that new job.

Carol had called me later to let us know that they had found Chris' wallet sticking out of the mud in the ravine. They decided to clean everything off the best they could and lay it all out to dry. They were very concerned that he only had a one dollar bill in his wallet.

That dollar bill was very important to Chris because it was signed. His Aunt Nancy and I had lost a bet on a card game to Chris and his Uncle Phil. The losers both had to autograph a dollar bill and give it to the winners. Chris always carried his bill in his wallet. Phil's signed dollar was framed and had a place on a shelf in his home. To say most everyone in our family is competitive is an understatement.

We knew there was so much to concentrate on. Even though it had only been a few days, Chris' lawn mowing business needed some attention. I had notified the business where Chris had been doing electrical work early on so they knew he had been in an accident and was in the hospital.

His lawn business contracts needed to be fulfilled so some friends and family had offered to pitch in. Somehow all the lawn contracts were covered for the rest of the summer. I kept track of his business, and continued with the billing and handling of the week to week scheduling for getting lawns mowed and keeping customers happy. This was not hard because Chris had been mowing most of his lawns for years so his clients were like extended family. They were all great and understood that he wasn't able to care for their lawns himself due to the accident, but that their lawn would be done. They were so supportive of Chris.

On June eighth, a police officer had come to see us at the hospital. They questioned us on the days leading up to the accident and to get Chris' blood test results. He had been one of the first officers at the scene so it was good to be able to thank him for what he had done for Chris. He helped take care of Chris before the ambulance arrived and we were told that someone, either an officer or early responder, drove the ambulance so the two paramedics could work on Chris. Chris had done his job to get himself to Carol's and Robert's house, everyone else was doing their job. Thankful!!

Jeff's family is a lot smaller than mine. His sister Paula and her husband Norm had already come to the hospital. Jeff had called his brother Al and his wife Judy on the first day, but they were living in

Tennessee so he told them not to come until we found out more on Chris' condition. Our daughter Amanda had taken it upon herself sometime on June seventh to call Uncle Al and Aunt Judy and told them her dad really needed them. Even though my nine brothers and sisters and most of their families had already been there and are extremely close with Jeff, there is nothing like your BIG BROTHER. When they arrived, Amanda met them in the parking lot and escorted them up to the NICU ward. Jeff was so touched and happy that they were there.

Jeff kept everything going at the hospital with Chris' progress. He was relentless. My husband and I have been together since 1972. We dated for six years, and were married in 1978. I fell in love with Jeff all over again when I saw how great he was advocating for Chris and holding us all together.

During Chris' early survival days, the nieces and friends had put together a couple of web pages, one on *'Facebook'*. They posted to one regularly to keep everyone informed about updates on his condition, and the other, *'BUILT TC TOUGH'*, was for friends and family to post their thoughts for Chris.

'BUILT TC TOUGH' POSTING – June 8th

Aunt Mary told me "If it wasn't for Chris' strength we wouldn't have a road to be traveling down. He has endured so we will endure for him as long as it takes! Thank you all for your support and prayers. We are truly witnessing a miracle."

Liz B

JOURNAL ENTRY – June 8th

Hey Little Brother,

Wow! You are absolutely remarkable. The last three days we have watched you fight like hell to let us know that you are here. Every movement makes us **SO** proud. We are all so lucky to have you here and I am waiting for you to wake up and tell me to be quiet because I am talking too loud and hurting your head. ☺ Jack misses you and we keep telling him that he and Uncle Bean are going to go fishing real soon. Fight like **hell** brother.

All my love – Amanda

JOURNAL ENTRY – June 8th

Hey T.C. it's your boy Howard. Me and 'Fifty' kept watch over your place last night. Everything is fine at home bud. It took us quite a while to find all of your hidden security. It looks like you're all set up in case there is an all-out critter attack at your place with every window covered. I almost clipped a doe coming out of your driveway. You look good today my man. You'll be out with 'The Wolfpack' hunting in no time. I love you Bean and I can't wait to be sitting on your porch livin' the 'high life' with you. I know it will be soon. You're still the T.C. even in a building full of doctors!

Love you man – Howard.

NOTE: To shed some light on acronyms or terms of endearment mentioned throughout this story, some of the 'nicknames' Chris/Christopher's family and friends had created for him over the years are listed here: Bean – T.C. – Uncle Bean – Prince Bean – Smurf – Buckmaster – Cuzzo – Kissyfur – Bean Pole, and others. What the 'nicknames' mean to those who had lovingly 'dubbed' him one or more of these titles is between them. Even the hospital staff had dubbed him Rambo.

Chapter 8 – Days Blur

Thursday – Day 4…Friday – Day 5…

June 9, 2011…June 10, 2011

So many things happened over the next few days. They kept running tests and decided to wait until the foreign objects in Chris' brain festered up or walled off so that they could remove them all at one time. It was explained to us as similar to getting a sliver in your finger. When your body creates puss between the sliver and the live tissue this would be called 'walling off.' They hoped that they could then remove the foreign objects out the same hole they entered with the least amount of disturbance to the rest of the brain.

They took the tubes out of Chris' mouth, did a tracheotomy, and added a feeding tube in Chris' stomach on June 9th. They drilled a hole called a 'port' into his head to keep relieving the pressure on his brain. Intracranial Pressure (ICP) was explained to me as the pressure in his brain that they were trying to keep below twenty-five. If it reached twenty-five and stayed there for five minutes, he would be considered brain dead. They could have lifted his skull to relieve the ICP, but for now the port was working. They kept rolling him over, cleaning him, and hoping for no further complications.

Things seemed to be happening at such a slow pace for Chris, but the body does amazing things in the recovery and healing process. They continually ran a tube down his throat to remove phlegm that kept building up in his windpipe. So many things were happening that many days our visits were cut short. The only time we left his side was during procedures.

I'm Chris' mom and not a medical expert, but I tried very hard to keep up with all of the medical terms. My husband and daughters were so much better at remembering the terms. All I knew was that that was my baby struggling to stay alive. My heart was heavy seeing so many people struggling with this ordeal.

We were also trying to stay current with so many decisions we had to make on Chris' business matters and keeping everything else going. Jeff's work contact was awesome and he knew he could put that on the back burner. I worked at a school and summer vacation had started that week so I had no worries there.

'Team Benear' was so strong today. So many family and friends showed up to offer support and love.

JOURNAL ENTRY – June 9th

Heeeeeey Cuzzo!

Liz, Amanda, and I just checked in at the 'NICU Inn', for clarification purposes that's the intensive care unit in the neurology quarters. You look amazing today, and are doing so well! God is on your side! TEAM BEAN! Lots of people were here today for you! Today was a good day! Love you so much. You are everyone's HERO! Can't wait to see you open those eyes and say Hey Danes - I love your face!

Love – Dana Michelle   ♡

P.S. You are a <u>Big effffin Deal</u>!

JOURNAL ENTRY – June 9th

It has been a long day buster! We did not get to see you much today because you had a few procedures done. They took the tubes out of your mouth, and added both the trach and the feeding tube in your stomach. They also checked to make sure that there are no clots in your legs. They are clear! You also were breathing on your own too! I am so proud of everything you have accomplished at this point already. You are a *fighter*. Today I ordered camo wristbands for all of us to wear. We are all here for you.

I love you brother – Amanda   ♡

JOURNAL ENTRY – June 9th

Hey Chris,

I couldn't sleep Wednesday night so I wrote you a poem. I love you so much and can't wait to talk to you! I wrote it in the next couple of pages. You are so special to me. I want you to know.

Love you *bud* – Dana

JOURNAL ENTRY – June 9th

We may never know what happened

on that hot summer night.

The only thing we know for sure is

he's putting up a hell of a fight.

God was there that night with Chris,

guiding him and keeping him safe.

He let Jesus take the wheel for Chris

so that we could again see his face.

All of our thoughts and all of our prayers,

we are asking of the man up above.

Chris is a hero and an inspiration to all,

he is really someone we all love.

People come in and people go out,

there have been tons of people here.

And at the end of this miraculous road,

we are all on the same team, 'Team Benear'!

We are fighting with you Christopher,

wanting you to just open your eyes.

We know that you will get better quick,

and soon you'll be giving us all those high fives.

We all love and care about you,

we'll be here for you until the end.

You are the best cousin, brother, nephew, and son,

you are always there to be anyone's friend.

So let us bow our heads in prayer,

please God continue to watch over our family.

Glory be to the Father and to the Son,

Chris means so much to us and to so many.

Love – Dana Michelle

JOURNAL ENTRY – June 9th

Hey Chris! You clean up nice! You have a strong will to survive. We are so blessed to be there in your time of need. We have your flashlight that you have to come to the house to get. Keep Fighting! The kids want to see you soon.

Love – Aunt Carol & Uncle Robert

'BUILT TC TOUGH' POSTING – June 9th

Hey Chris! I'm so honored and proud to call you my cousin although I feel like you are more like a brother. Your strength is amazing, and I am looking forward to having you back.

Missing you like crazy. Missing you giving my mom a hard time, she is really missing that. There's no one who can do it quite the way you do!! ☺

Love you!! – Liz B

'BUILT TC TOUGH' POSTING – June 9th

Keep fightin' the fight Chris! You are our backbone! We can't wait to hear you talk the talk, only you know how! We love you bud!!!!

Cynda B

'BUILT TC TOUGH' POSTING – June 9th

TC! I know u didn't fight this whole way for nothin' bro! Hurry up and get better! We need our main wingman back!!

Ben N

'BUILT TC TOUGH' POSTING – June 9th

You certainly have taken the phrase "Out of the Woods" to a whole new level. So much so, from here on I will only be able to use it when telling your amazing story. After the fight you have had (and continue to have), you have left us all in awe of your strength and your courage to live. I can't thank you enough for putting up the fight to stay with us…life just wouldn't be the same without my Kissyfur!

Emily B

'BUILT TC TOUGH' POSTING – June 9th

Hey Chris,

We love u and u are in our prayers, even little Maretta's! You are a part of our family and my girls love u! You are so tough! Continue prayers for u, love u! All the Finleys!

Laura F

'BUILT TC TOUGH' POSTING – June 9th

Hey Chris!

I can't believe the determination and will to live that you have shown these past few days. I feel like the word "inspiration" cannot be overused. You are truly amazing and I am so proud of you and happy to be part of your family. I never thought I'd say this, but I can't wait to hear your voice. I love you.

Stacy H

'BUILT TC TOUGH' POSTING – June 9th

Hey Chris!

You're an amazing man and loved by so many. Soon, you will open those big eyes and see all of the people who are rooting for you. We know that you will heal in record time, because you...are Chris Benear! You are in our thoughts and prayers Chris!!!

Love – Jeff and Sue P

'BUILT TC TOUGH' POSTING – June 9th

Keep fighting Chris! I love you so much brother! You are an amazing role model for everyone! Please believe me when I say people know your story! People in the hospital who don't even know you know your story! Well because YOU ARE A BIG EFFIN DEAL AROUND HERE! I look up to you so much, I always have. I'm proud to say you're my cousin!

IF GOD WILL BRING YOU TO IT, HE'LL BRING YOU THRU IT! FIGHTING WITH CHRIS! LET'S GO!

♡ Dana Michelle W

Friday

June 10, 2011

What a roller coaster we were on then. In the morning it could be good news, two hours later it could be iffy. Good, bad, iffy, scary, scary, scary.

Dr. Yang and Jeff were at the desk in the intensive care unit (ICU). She was explaining to Jeff how the foreign objects in Chris' head had come together like they had hoped and that surgery would be a lot easier now. So finally she had given Jeff some good news. Jeff gave her a BIG hug. Everyone around the ICU stopped and stared because seeing Dr. Yang hug a family member of one of her patients didn't happen very often. I was in the room with Chris, but I was told by more than one eye-witness that the HUG was very sincere by both parties.

When I first met my husband Jeff, he was not a hugger, but over the years of being around me and my family, hugging has become more comfortable to him. In my family when you leave to go somewhere, you hug…when you haven't seen someone in a while, you hug…when you get good news, you HUG…

That day we felt so much love and support. The waiting room down the hall which had become our home away from home had been busy all day. We kept someone in with Chris at all times and tried to get everyone a few minutes to say hi to him. We didn't know how much Chris understood, but we were sure he heard every word being said. People were always asking if we needed anything.

All we really needed was for Chris to wake up and come back to us. One day my friend Cathy V called and said that she and her husband Ted were coming to visit. She asked, "What do you need?" "Socks," I stated. Not sure why I was so worried about socks because I was going home tomorrow, but I was only wearing my shoes when I went in to see Chris and had no slippers. Socks would have been great. Cathy brought me socks.

JOURNAL ENTRY – June 10th

Chris,

I know I've told you a hundred times I LOVE YOU. I feel guilty that I didn't pay more attention to the last week or so when you mentioned how tired you were. I don't know what happened to you and why your truck left the road. All we can think is that it was because you were so tired from working and being out in the extreme heat.

Alex and I went and looked at the path you had to take from where your truck stopped to where you got help at Carol's and Robert's house. You have always amazed me with your determination your whole life. This time was no different in how you were able to make it that far in your condition. Jenny B-A said she had a dream that seven angels helped show you the way. I bet I can guess who the angels might have been. When you needed to rest they sat down beside you and waited. Monday morning was the worst morning of my life, driving to Ann Arbor not knowing whether I would ever talk to my son again.

When we arrived you were in very bad shape. It was so hard for all of us to see you that way. It seemed like Mom and I no sooner got there when I turned around and Uncle David was there for me. I know he was as scared as I was. Alex and Steph got there…it was so bad we didn't know if you were going to make it. Now we are approaching the end of Day 5 – 3:50 p.m., it has been a long five days.

Chris, you can't imagine the friends and family that have been here to pray for you and support us as a family. I have never cried so many tears in my whole life…or said so many prayers…or hugged so many hugs. Yesterday you had a good morning. Heather and Steph spent the night with you and you were making some sounds that were encouraging. Then your trach and feeding tube were installed yesterday. Your temperature went up to 101 degrees and your brain pressure went up. Not a good night. We're in it for the long haul.

Love – Dad

'BUILT TC TOUGH' POSTING – 3:11 June 10th

We finally got some good news! All of your blood draws came back clean. No signs of infections. God is working overtime this week! Keep praying.

Chris, I love you – Amanda

JOURNAL ENTRY – June 10th

Christopher,

You know you can't keep me away. As always I am supporting you and in awe of what a strong guy you always are. So proud of you.

Keep fighting. You're always a winner. Everyone is praying and cheering you on.

You go!!

    We all love you – Linda M B

JOURNAL ENTRY – June 10th

Your legs and knees and arms were x-rayed today…no broken bones, but some soft tissue damage. Dad and Dr. Yang actually hugged today (they didn't hit it off so well when they first met Monday morning). She said the 'foreign material' in your head has gotten smaller and came together in one spot…which is great news. ☺ You had a big day yesterday, so you need your rest today to recover!

    I love you brother ☺ – Steph

JOURNAL ENTRY – June 10th

My joke now is I'm part of the Benear family because I am here so much. ☺ I delivered cards and a poster to Mary from the students and staff at Howell High School (HHS).

Keep on fighting Chris – you should see all the people here who love you! What a family you are part of. I am going to rent out Uncle Buffalo for parties... ☺

Love – Jen G

JOURNAL ENTRY – June 10th

Hey Chris,

There definitely is only one person in the world that could get through an accident like that! You are unbelievable! I am so happy that you put up such a fight! You have been making more and more progress every day in the hospital. I can't wait until the day you can go up north with us. I will warn you – I will beat you on the four wheelers and in euchre! Just kidding – I will let you win!! Keep getting better!

Love ya – Jen A

(Matt is praying for you every day! He is as worried as I am!)

'BUILT TC TOUGH' POSTING – June 10th

We pray for your quick recovery every day Chris! I am amazed at the strength you have shown so far, you are truly amazing. I never thought I would be telling you how much I miss you giving me a hard time, but here it is! So you are allowed to do that forever and I won't be mad!

Jenn A

'BUILT TC TOUGH' POSTING – June 10th

Good morning Chris! On my way to work this morning I heard "Something to be Proud of". You, your determination, your desire to win and never give up are something I am very proud of. Keep fighting and know that we are all with you every step of the way.

Love you! – Liz B

'BUILT TC TOUGH' POSTING – June 10th

I used to love how Em always called you Kissyfur, so much so that I had my own Christopher. And while my little man has always been Christopher to me, he knows exactly who Kissyfur is thanks to Em. That's how great your family's love for you is— they can't help but talk about you all the time. I feel so blessed to be able to tell others about the miracles God has been working in you. I am praying constantly that he continues to heal you and bring you back to your family and friends. It has been amazing to see the number of people out there praying for your recovery, people who have never even met you or your family! With the enormous circle of family and friends around you, I am not at all surprised at your desire to keep fighting. We're all praying God keeps giving you the strength for the battle. Keep fighting Chris!

Ali K

'BUILT TC TOUGH' POSTING – June 10th

Christopher – we have been through a whole lot together in the last 23 years of being buds, a lot of ups and downs. If I have learned anything, it is that you are a fighter and you love your family and friends very much. You will get through this with flying colors because of your strength and determination. I know you aren't going to give up! Looking forward to talking to you again… P.S. Big John says he is ready to whoop you in another game of ping pong again!

Sarah V

Chapter 9 – Days Pass

Saturday – Day 6…Sunday – Day 7…Monday – Day 8

June 11, 2011…June 12, 2011…June 13, 2011

Chris had been improving every day which was great news. The doctors were encouraged by his progress and we were all blown away by his determination to get back to being 'The Bean or T.C.'.

The lawns were getting mowed and 'Team Benear' was going strong. Jeff and I had started walking by ourselves every once in a while to get a little breather. Some days we would never even talk; just walk hand in hand for ten minutes or so. That day we found ourselves walking down by the children's section of the U of M hospital. It broke our hearts as we watched those young families and their little children, not knowing if they were fighting for their life or just having a medical setback. We would smile and say hi and we were always greeted with a smile or a wave back. You can always find someone worse off than you. It gave us the strength we needed to keep going for our son.

We waited for Chris' computerized axial tomography (CAT) scan to come back with some good news, hopefully. We needed some good news. It was so difficult watching Chris suffering and everyone who cares for him hurting.

JOURNAL ENTRY – June 11th

Kissyfur,

I don't think you really know how much you mean to me. This week has by far been the worst week of my life…that is until today. I came to see you Monday night and couldn't stop looking at you in amazement. You have fought so hard to stay with us and we couldn't be more grateful for your continued fight.

Going back to Chicago, I counted down the hours until I could see you again. When I got back here today though, I was able to see all of your improvements. You even squeezed my hand!! Gosh did that feel good! You're moving both sides and starting to make a facial expression or two. You sure are <u>amazing</u>! Finding the words is just close to impossible.

Okay we need to talk! You just flipped me off! You're in big trouble Kissyfur!

♡ Emily Eileen

JOURNAL ENTRY – June 11th

Hey Chris!

It has taken me all week to write in here and I am still quite speechless. I really am having a difficult time realizing that this is actually happening, although I am staying very strong and positive. I am in absolute awe of your strength and determination! I guess I will try to tell you what's been going on while you have been resting-fighting-inspiring – you have really inspired so many people!

So Monday, June 6 in the afternoon was the first time I was able to visit you. I wasn't sure what to expect except I knew you had put up the fight of your life to stay with us.

There were so many people in the waiting room and hallway when I got here; a true testament to the wonderful person you are and the great support system you have.

Tuesday, June 7, I stayed the night. I had the two a.m. to five a.m. shift. I tried to just be quiet and let you rest. Part way through the night you gave me quite a scare. Just as I dozed off, you moved your left leg and arm…a lot. I didn't know if you were supposed to move or if you were going to flash me, they only had you covered with a little loin cloth. ☺

I left for work Wednesday morning and came back about 6 p.m. Wednesday night and you looked so much better. It was a great sign, and once again you amazed all of us with your will to get back to us so quickly. Thursday, June 9, I came back after work and stayed the night with your Mom and Dad. Once again you were looking better than the day before. Your room was freezing cold. I am not sure how your Dad wasn't an ice block by the morning.

You had a computerized axial tomography scan (CAT scan) today, will find out results soon. Friday you had another great day. It was girls' night at the 'NICU Inn'. Amanda, Emily, Stephanie, and I all stayed the night. Emily was so thankful to make it back to see you; it was good bonding time for all us girls with our 'Kissyfur'. Saturday morning, June 11, Nate F was your first visitor and you recognized his voice and were able to look at him with a little eye opening assistance from Steph. You were able to move your right arm across your body. What a great sight and great feeling for everyone! You even looked at me today! I could see that you were in there and I was so grateful to see you again! Love you and your strength. Thanks for getting back to us.

Sunday, June 12, you really needed your rest today so we tried to be quiet. The brain pressure was stable, but there were concerns so we just let you rest. Emily spent the day with you then headed back to Chicago. The CAT scan showed the 'foreign material' getting smaller and moving closer together, good news. You are still fighting so hard and we are so thankful for that. Talk to you again soon.

Love you – Liz

JOURNAL ENTRY – June 11th

Smurf - Rambo

I hope that you know how many people really love you and care for you. You would not believe just how many people have been up here to see you! Every time I'm here it is standing room only in the waiting room and people spilling out into the hallway. I hope that you can feel the love coming from everyone. Please hurry back to us!

Love – Ronda

JOURNAL ENTRY – June 11th

So proud of you today. You squeezed my hand when I told you that Vande was here…and not the tickle me with a good time show me one!

Sarah V

Sunday

June 12, 2011

It was an extremely hard day that day. The doctors asked for there to be very few visitors. Chris needed as much rest and quiet time as he could get so we passed the word that visitors would be limited. People understood. That day was a Sunday one week after Chris' accident, but the waiting room was still full and everyone understood. It definitely helped when the girls posted on Chris' web page on

'*Facebook*' that visitors would be really limited the next couple of days. Friends and family still showed up with treats, meals, and lots of hugs, but they understood they probably wouldn't get to see Chris. Only a few did get in to see him.

Father Dave came from Saint Joseph parish in Howell today to visit with us. I had never met Father Dave before this because we had switched and started to go to a new parish when Father Rahrig had retired from Saint Joseph. Father Rahrig was our priest. He married my mom and dad, baptized me, and then married me and Jeff. My children had all gone to Saint Joseph Catholic School. Father Rahrig had baptized all three of them as well as my husband Jeff in 1995. When he retired, my mom decided to go to a new parish and I followed.

I was in with Chris when someone came down and informed me Father Dave, who was relatively new to Saint Joseph, was there looking for us. I had walked down to our 'Inn' and Father Dave explained that a family friend of ours had told him about Chris' accident. He asked if he could pray with Chris and for him. We went to the bedside and he placed his hand on Chris and prayed for him then led us all in prayer. It was so emotional and peaceful. As I walked Father Dave back to the elevator we talked about what had happened. He couldn't explain to me why this accident had happened to our son, but said to trust in our faith in God to help us get through this difficult time. He left telling us he would continue to pray for all of us and if we needed anything to give him a call even if it was just to talk. We had needed prayers and his presence that day.

JOURNAL ENTRY – June 12th

Chris

Hey buddy, you really look so much better today. Bill bought you a deck of cards and some cigars. He's going to practice Euchre so he can be worthy of being your partner. I'm really proud of you. We had some deer in our backyard this morning and of course we thought of you. (Don't let it go to your head.☺)

Bill and Alex cut lawns all day Saturday for you. Of course Bill has some funny stories for you. ☺ Keep fighting sweetie.

We are all praying for you – ♡ Heather (Apple70)

Monday

June 13, 2011

Last night and this morning were so hard. They had trouble relieving the pressure on Chris' brain and everyone was worried. They informed us they *would* do surgery tomorrow, June 14, at 4:00 p.m.

We were really limiting the time anyone was in with Chris. He needed his rest so there was no talking while you were in the room.

The day progressed so slowly. We kept in touch with the doctors and they were sure tomorrow's surgery was the right decision. They said that the foreign objects in Chris' brain had walled off and they would hopefully remove them with as little disturbance to the rest of the brain as possible.

We spent most of the afternoon and early evening in our little corner of the hospital NICU waiting room. We continued to keep the visiting very limited and tried to just keep everyone's spirits up.

As we were in the waiting room, the doctor who was to do surgery at 4:00 p.m. the next day happened to walk by our little 'NICU Inn' and Jeff noticed him. Jeff said, "You headed out Doc?" "Yes," he replied. "Okay, straight home sir and get lots of sleep we really need you on your 'A' game tomorrow," Jeff said. Doc smiled and left.

Our daughter Amanda is a lawyer so she set me up with a lawyer this afternoon to start the process of getting guardianship and conservator over Chris. We needed to pay bills and make some decisions we hadn't even thought about yet.

So many people were there to help us get through the evening.

JOURNAL ENTRY – June 13th

Chris, I am so scared about surgery tomorrow. I have to say I don't think I have ever been so afraid of anything in my life. I remember when we got the bad news about your anterior cruciate ligament and found out you wouldn't be able to play football and how bad you felt and we both cried. This is so scary!

Love – Dad

JOURNAL ENTRY – June 13th

Hey Christopher! Jodi and I spent the night with Steph here in the waiting room. We didn't get to spend any of it with you this time. You needed some rest, so we had to settle for holding your hand in spirit only. I brought something to read to you. At first I thought a romance novel, you know so you can get some pointers, ☺ but I took pity on you and brought you a "Deer and Deer Hunting" magazine instead. It's not exactly riveting to me, but you might enjoy it. There's an article called "Magic Beans". At first I thought it was about you, but it turns out it's about soybeans. (Did you know that soybean pods are high in protein and fat, making them a good nutrition source for deer late in the season?) Soon I might know more about this stuff than you!

I got to see you briefly this morning, and though your right leg looks a bit rough still, the rest of you is looking better. It's going to be a long road, but you have me (and tons of others) to help you get through this. When you're up for it, I'll quiz you on all of this new stuff we read on deer hunting!

Love you! – Stacy

P.S. Was just reading "7 Food Plot Rules My Grandpa Taught Me."

There's one for soybeans and since I just mentioned them above, I thought I'd just jot it down for you. "Don't plant soybeans until you can pull down your trousers and sit in the soil for one minute." Maybe when you get better, we can try it out. And by 'we', I mean you! ☺

JOURNAL ENTRY – June 13th

Chris

I'm praying for you. I love you! I know God will give you the power to get better. Tomorrow God will be with you so just relax and let him help you. It's going to take a little time, but you'll get better and be back to your old self.

I love you Chris – Amelia B

JOURNAL ENTRY – June 13th

Chris

Hey couzzo, I'm here waiting for you. You know you're my brother when Dave's away and it always makes my day. I'm waiting for you to walk in the door and say hello again. I know you will. I have had my orange 'Crocs' on for you, and will always. I know people give you some crazy looks for them, but I'm sporting them still.

'Katie, Katie, Katie' is all I hear you saying in my mind these days. Of all the things I want to do with you, playing pool tops them all, relaxing and visiting, and racking the balls. The dance floor is waiting for you to join us again. I will love you always brother.

– Katelyn

JOURNAL ENTRY – June 13th

Hi Chris,

What a week. You are one tough person and everyone is so proud of you! You're working so hard, you have so many people praying for you. You have had a full house since you arrived. You'd be so proud of your family too. Stephanie and Amanda are taking such good care of your mom and dad.

They're going to get some things started tomorrow (surgery) so you'll be working hard again. God will be there with you. Life has given you a quick turn, but everything will all work out. It's going to take time, but you'll get there. You have your own '*Facebook*' page. You also have lots of pretty Nurses taking extra special care of you. Talk to you soon Chris!

Love – Linda B

Chapter 10 – Long Hard Night and Day

Tuesday – Day 9

June 14, 2011

Barbara had been the Nurse on the evening of June 13 in charge of Chris. She had so much trouble keeping his ICP down. Doctors were in and out, medication changes were made, and his brain swelling was still staying high.

Jeff and I kept rotating in and out, but it was so hard seeing the worry on everyone's faces. Again I remembered being told that if the pressure stayed up at 25 for five minutes, he would be considered brain dead. My heart sank every time it was even close to that mark. Barbara was sweating because she was so busy working with Chris. We had the pleasure of having Barbara for his nurse quite a few times, and I could see in her eyes how concerned she was.

In the early morning hours, Liz came in to relieve us for a little while. Chris had a portable CAT scan around 5:30 a.m., the results were not good. Liz had come down to the waiting room and told Jeff and me that they needed us to come and sign papers.

When we arrived, they told us that as soon as they could gather the whole team, they would be taking Chris in for Surgery. The doctor told Jeff the papers needed to be signed. Jeff really struggled to sign those papers. I could see him physically shaking he was so worried about the surgery. The doctor put his hand on Jeff's shoulder and told us they would take good care of Chris. With Amanda by his side, he signed.

We were all by the door when they wheeled Chris out into the hallway. We told him we loved him and that we would be waiting right there for him. They had informed us that we should hear from them between 12 p.m. and 1 p.m. It was around 6:30 a.m. when they left with Chris.

Talk about a long and excruciating morning. That wait was something that really tried your faith and patience.

I can't even tell you who was there or how we made it through those next hours. Everything had become a blur until Jeff saw Dr. Yang coming down the hallway. He met her and escorted her to all of us around 10:30 a.m. She told us everything went as good as it could go and she was very optimistic. Jeff gave her a HUG. She informed us that they were going to put Chris in an induced coma for a couple of days so his brain had time to recover.

Chris was brought back up to the NICU fourth floor a while after his surgery. We spent as much time in his room as we could. He seemed to be resting peacefully even with all the IVs and wrapping around his head. During all that time even the wounds on his legs had seemed to be healing. A lot of family and friends heard about the surgery and just wanted to be there. Chris' visitors were kept to just a few during the afternoon, but the waiting room was 'Team Benear' strong all day.

Jeff and I left the hospital feeling confident that Chris was in good hands. The sisters were going to stay with a small posse of girls so we had decided to do a few errands and make a needed trip home. We still had no idea how Chris would be after the surgery, but the doctors had seemed to be optimistic about his recovery.

After a few errands I had dropped Jeff off at home to look at one of Chris' lawn mowers and I had paid my mom a visit. Talk about hugs, there is nothing like a hug from your mom. My mom had raised ten children and worked out of the house for years after we were grown up. When we were growing up on the farm, she had done everything she could to make us feel like we had everything we needed. We had followed in her footsteps to do the same for our children.

We had everything we needed; a home, food, and lots of love. Mom knew Chris was worse off than what she had been told so she was so grateful I stopped by. I explained to her as much as I could about what was happening with him without being too alarming about

Chris' recovery expectations. I was honest and told her that we wouldn't know what his limitations would be or what his future held until Chris woke up from the induced coma. We still needed all the prayers we could get. My mom was great at <u>praying</u>. As I headed home from my mom's, I thought about going to see my Aunt Joyce.

My Aunt Joyce is my mom's brother's wife. We had been very close to Aunt Joyce and her husband Tom for a long time and had been helping out with many different activities and projects around their property. Chris had a special relationship with his Aunt Joyce. Their mutual love of the Detroit Tigers, betting on Michigan vs Michigan State games in any sport, and their mutual love of animals and the outdoors had created a special bond. Since Uncle Tom had passed, Chris and his dad were Aunt Joyce's right hand men for electrical projects, tree trimming, lawn mowing, and the fixing of anything they could handle. I had tried to keep in touch with Aunt Joyce every day or two to let her know how Chris was progressing. She was so worried about Chris. A phone call would ease her mind a little bit. She would have to wait awhile for a visit, so a call would have to do, since my visit with my mom had drained me.

JOURNAL ENTRY – June 14th

Hi Christopher

It's Tuesday morning around 7 a.m. I just missed you going into surgery. I know you're going to breeze through surgery like everything else you do. I will be back to see you soon. Dale said when I left home to tell you 'hi' from him.

We love ya! – Linda B

P.S. I forgot to tell you the other day…sorry about the pink…flowers. I knew you would get a chuckle.

JOURNAL ENTRY – June 14th

Hey Chris,

I spent a little time with you this morning, so glad I was able to. About 5:45 a.m. they performed a portable CAT scan and by about 6:20 a.m. they were rushing you off for surgery; which was the best decision ever! ☺ Not only did you get finished one and a half hours early, the surgery was successful.

I knew it would be. Seriously, I have not doubted you or your strength to get through this at any point. I feel blessed to have seen you before and I am looking forward to seeing you in just a little while. I am going to wear my "burnt orange" Lewiston sweatshirt every day I see you just because I know you will recognize it immediately. It has been a long, but very encouraging week and I look forward to the weeks ahead, your recovery, and getting to hang with you again soon.

Love you Lots! – Liz ♡

JOURNAL ENTRY – June 14th

Hi Brother!

Wow! You were absolutely <u>amazing</u> today. I am so proud of your strength and continued determination and will. It was a really long morning waiting for the docs to come back and tell us how surgery went. They said it went good. Five pieces of wood, almost three inches long <u>each</u>.

There is no one else I know strong enough to take this. We will beat this and be so much stronger.

    I love you – Amanda

JOURNAL ENTRY – June 14th

Buckmaster – you just had surgery and you did great! We are so proud of you budd! We are all wearing bracelets that Amanda ordered which say "Fighting with Chris." You can do it hunnie!

    Love – Heather

JOURNAL ENTRY – June 14th

T.C., Good job today bud. You got me out of work again today!! You know I appreciate that! You are an amazing guy and someone I look up to. I can't wait to have a 'Highlife' and catch some fish with you Cuz.

    I love U Man – Howard

JOURNAL ENTRY – June 14th

Hey Brother!

I haven't written in here too often as I'd rather spend my time questioning your nurses and keeping up on all your numbers…which by the way, I think I'm halfway there to being an NICU Nurse ☺. I am so proud of you every single day. You are and will forever be my hero! I always have looked up to you so much and miss hanging out and riding around on your tractor pulling out trees! You are like my second half and things are just not the same without hearing from you every day…we are so much alike and I miss you buddy. Your surgery went really good today and I'm staying the night with you to be sure everything goes good…we have to keep up our good track record, we seem to do well together! I'll be holding your hand soon…

Love you so much ☺ – Steph

JOURNAL ENTRY – June 14th

Hey Stud

I'm sure you're pretty sick of hearing how bad ass you are, but you've earned the title "Super Dooper Bad Ass Bean." ☺

I'm staying the night tonight to keep you and your sisters company. Dana is here too. I've been downloading songs that remind me of you. I'm going to make a playlist so you can jam in your room.

I was able to go back to hold your hand a few times today, which made me very happy, especially considering what you went through today. Everyone is fighting over the pieces of wood that were pulled out. I kindly explained we'd put them in a showcase in your pool room next to the twins. LOL

Well, Amanda is exhausted so lights are going off soon.

Love ya lots – see ya in the a.m.! – Nessie

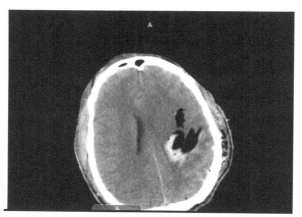

Chris' CT Scan wood location

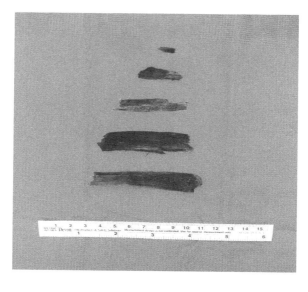

Pieces of wood pulled from Chris' Brain

Chapter 11 – The Waiting Game

Wednesday – Day 10

June 15, 2011

We headed back to the hospital on Wednesday morning. It had been eleven days since our son's accident, but this drive was a little easier. Yes, we still have many unanswered questions, but Chris' determination and will to survive is giving us the chance to bring our son home.

In an ideal life, you should never have to lose a child. I've seen the devastation and heartbreak of family and friends that have had to endure the loss of a child. I am sure no words I expressed or hugs I gave could ease their pain, but maybe at that time caring words and loving hugs helped them get through those first seriously rough weeks. Without our family and friends those first eleven days would have been so much more excruciating. It was so incredible having so much support.

When we arrived at the hospital we found out that Chris had just been taken down for another CAT scan, and his night had been a little rough.

They had kept Chris medicated so that his body had a good chance to heal. Rest was the most important thing for him at that point.

The CAT scan had come back with good results, and the doctors were very optimistic that all foreign objects were removed.

Visitors were kept to a minimum and were only able to visit with Chris for a few minutes at a time. Jeff and I or the girls stayed in the room all day, and there were no conversations happening. We kept the room as quiet as possible so as not to disturb his healing.

We are so blessed to have so many people that really care about Chris. I spent most of that day trying to make sure everyone knew Chris' surgery went well. There were lots of phone calls to return and messages to text back, but the diversion really helped. At certain times it was good to be kept busy.

I spent the night with Chris, we all hoped he would have a very peaceful night.

JOURNAL ENTRY – June 15th

Gooooood Moorrnninnggg ROCKSTAR !   Just telling you this a.m. that I love to love you! You are amazing!   Keep up the outstanding work!   Every day is a new day you are moving mountains! Let's give 'em something to talk about! The sun is shining this a.m. and I can't wait to see you when you get back from your CAT scan. So we can hang!

Love you cuzzo! – ♡ Dana Michelle

JOURNAL ENTRY – 3:30 p.m. June 15th

Hey there big guy. Still here waiting for you to wake up. Take as long as you need. You've got some healing to do. It's amazing how many people have been in and out of this hospital to visit you and support your mom, dad, and sisters. We all love you buddy, and are pulling for you. Get better soon. I'm actually getting the urge to play some spades or hearts.

Love you – Aunt Paula

JOURNAL ENTRY – 7:30 p.m. June 15th

Beans,

Bains here again. Muffs and I just came down to check to see how your surgery went. Obviously you pulled through great, as expected! They have you asleep for a couple of days so you can rest so unfortunately I can't tell you any good stories, but it's probably a good thing right now. They don't want you to get all riled up and what not.

You're doing as well as possible right now. You wouldn't believe how many people are praying for you man, everybody you know and tons of people that have just heard about it that you don't even know. You're a strong SOB Beans, but we already knew that, LOL!

Well, keep on fighting brother. We love you man, and can't wait for this to be over. Even though I've seen you, your truck, and the crash site, it still seems almost like it's not real…just a bad dream, but unfortunately it's not.

Bains

JOURNAL ENTRY – June 15th

Hi Chris,

We've been up to see you and there's not a day that goes by that we don't think about you, pray for you, and shed a tear. We love you Buddy!!! You mean a lot to us! You've always meant a lot to ME!! You're a special young man with a lot of people who care about you. Donnie thinks you're just the "MAN."

Get better sweetheart!

We love you – Don and Aunt Sharon

Chapter 12 – Time to Rest

Thursday – Day 11

June 16, 2011

Test results kept coming back positive so everyone was really encouraged. Chris' vitals were good and had been staying strong so they might cut back on his meds the next day. It had been eleven days since Chris' accident, and his leg wounds were healing nicely. At that point, they were not sure if he would need skin grafts. The decision would be made later on down the recovery road.

We continued to keep visitors to very limited time in Chris' room. He seemed to be very comfortable that day and we hoped that he would be coming out of the induced coma soon. I had taken advantage of that time of rest to catch up on bills and schedules for Chris' lawns. Linda B had brought me an expandable file case so I could keep things organized away from home and wow did that come in handy. I tried to keep track of insurance papers, scheduled appointments, and it seemed like we constantly filled out forms for one thing or another.

'BUILT TC TOUGH' POSTING – June 16th

Good morning Chris! I stayed last night with Kate and your parents. All of your pressures came down last night! You are getting some much needed rest and will continue to do so for the next couple of days. I look forward to seeing you this weekend! I know it's only a matter of time before we get to see you open those beautiful eyes again. Keep on fighting; we are with you every step of the way!

Love you – Elizabeth B

JOURNAL ENTRY – June 16th

Hey Bean Pole

Corn Dog here, saw you sleepin' in bed. Hope you're dreaming about that Big Buck!

Mark C

JOURNAL ENTRY – 10:33 p.m. June 16th

Chris

You never cease to <u>AMAZE</u> me! When they say something cannot be done, you prove them wrong. When they say it won't happen, you show them it will. Every day is a new day and you are showing and proving that better than anyone ever has! (I'm just a little prejudiced.) I'm so proud of you! I'm thanking God every day for the miracles you've made thus far!

Keep movin' mountains buddy!

Let's give 'em something to talk about! xoxo

Love you – Dana Michelle

Chapter 13 – Good Days

Friday – Day 12…Saturday – Day 13…Sunday – Day 14…
Monday – Day 15…

June 17, 2011…June 18, 2011…June 19, 2011…Jun 20, 2011

They started to take some medications away that day to see how Chris would react. His vitals had stayed positive, and he had even tried to move and blink his eyes. <u>Awesome news</u>.

Kiel mowed Chris' lawn that day and weed whipped all the weeds down the length of the driveway. Chris would be so thankful that everything was getting done for him, and it had taken so much pressure off the rest of us. All of our focus could be on Chris' healing.

Vanessa had informed us about a fundraiser and silent auction they were getting together. She was so excited about a CD she had put together of around twenty songs – Hank, Garth, Toby, Luke and more. They were designing a t-shirt to sell and the CDs were gifts. They had already taken in some donations for the silent auction. I was so humbled by the support our family was being shown by so many people. We are blessed.

JOURNAL ENTRY – 10:30 a.m. June 17th

Hey Chris (Dad here)…It's no surprise to me how hard it is to do things around our house and your house without you there. I am so used to you helping me make good decisions on what is the best way to do things. Cynda, Robert, and Tigger all stopped the other night and weeded our garden, it looks great.

I can't wait until you're there to help eat those fresh cucumbers and coleslaw. Allen and Judy have been with us the last few days. They are among so many other people who are pulling for your full recovery.

You have always amazed me with your ability to achieve great things when you put forth your inner strength. I don't expect this step backwards in your life will be any different. Mom and I are prepared to do whatever it takes to get you back to full status.

I am still trying to troubleshoot your mower. Yesterday Allen and Norm helped remove the fuel petcock and made sure everything was clean. Norm changed the blades and Al ran to town and got some clamps. Hopefully, Alex and Steph won't have any more issues with it for a while.

Today all of your numbers look good. We are hoping that by the end of next week we will be talking to you once again.

Love – Your Dad

JOURNAL ENTRY – June 17th

Hey Chris

I don't really know where to start! I can't imagine what it has been like for you over the past few weeks. You are very fortunate to have such a great family and a tight knit group of friends. This will be a hell of a good story that you can tell James and Annie when they get a little older. I can't wait until November rolls around to get away up to the cabin for some huntin' and some Tally burgers. I wish I could be here every day with you, but you are in my prayers every day! Hang in there buddy. You are an inspiration and a <u>fighter</u>.

The Scott family loves you! – Marv

JOURNAL ENTRY – June 17th

Hey Chris

This is a quick note to say hi. We saw you move and blink, and it made your Dad so hopeful and happy. We are thinking of you and praying for your recovery. You hang in there and we'll be back to see you soon. You are strong, have survived, and will recover. We'll be here to support you and your family through it all.

We love you – Jessica B

Saturday

June 18, 2011

Had a few visitors that day who said it was nice to see Jeff and me smiling. Chris was slowly coming out of the coma so we were finally getting the chance to see his beautiful eyes. We couldn't tell exactly what he was thinking, but he seemed to be trying to focus on us and his surroundings.

JOURNAL ENTRY – June 18th

Chris, as you are still fighting we are still praying. We have faith you will fight like hell.

We love you – Sarah P

JOURNAL ENTRY – June 18th

Hey Chris

This is a special day for me – one reason is that I get to see you awake for the first time. That is my birthday present from you. Yes, today is my birthday! Can't wait to get you back home so we can sit by the pool and have a tall cool one together. I've said many prayers for you Bud. I'll be back to see you soon!

Your good buddy – Ron M

Sunday – Father's Day

June 19, 2011

So many visitors arrived that day with so much love for Chris. Everyone was so excited about the news of Chris opening his eyes, and that he had seemed to be coming around.

Tests had come back with positive news and doctors were very encouraged. We still have no idea what functions, if any, Chris has lost or if he would have limitations going forward. What we did know for sure was that he had moved mountains in the last two weeks.

That Father's Day was not our typical Father's Day celebration. We were so thankful for all of our children being there for their dad, and for all the love from our friends and family, taking time to visit with us as part of their Father's Day activity meant more to us than they could possibly know.

JOURNAL ENTRY – June 19th

Good Morning Christopher!

I spent the night here at the suite of the 'NICU Inn' with Steph and Emily. I was able to sit with you for a couple of hours in the wee hours of the morning. You are looking better and better. You had your eyes open and seemed to be wide awake.

I think that you're resting this morning to make up for it. I can't wait to see what you can do next! See you soon.

Love ya! – Stacy

JOURNAL ENTRY – June 19th

Hi Christopher!

It's Sarah – I just wanted to tell you hi, and how much I miss you! You are truly a fighter, and amazing to me and all of your friends/family. I am praying for you non-stop and you are <u>ALWAYS</u> in my thoughts.

Funny story – I went in to see you with your dad. I felt a little light- headed, and left after talking to you. Your dad asked me why I left and I said because if Chris sees me faint in front of him, he will never let me live that one down. ☺

Your family is amazing. They are so strong. Keep pushing bud – I can't wait until you are better and we can go to my cottage and we can do all the stuff you have always talked about. I love you buddy – you are amazing, and I can't wait to talk to you.

L♡ve – Sarah

JOURNAL ENTRY – June 19th

Hey Chris!

You are a fighter! I love you so much, and I can't even imagine fighting as much as you are! Keep strong and keep fighting! You never gave up on us, so we won't give up on you!

Andrew

JOURNAL ENTRY – 9:45 p.m. June 19th

Hey Buddy!

I was finally able to come back and see you. I went home for a few days to spend some time with Jack and Kate. They miss Uncle Bean so much. Jack asked yesterday when he was going bear hunting with Uncle Bean. I told him that you were just waiting a *little* longer until they were really big. He thought that was cool. I was able to see you blink and open your eyes today. It was wonderful. Now I just want to hear your <u>VOICE</u>. I love you and miss you so much.

I love you with all I have – Amanda

JOURNAL ENTRY – 10:30 p.m. June 19th

Kissyfur – I finally figured out how to spell it like 'Emmers.' ☺

Your big beautiful eyes were open lots today. It's so amazing to see you looking around.

I brought that Cuban cigar I promised you. It's a little Father's Day present for your dad. He's excited to be able to smoke it with you in the barn. When I told you about it today, you were moving your legs like crazy. We could tell you were excited for it too.

I'm spending the night tonight with the 'fam'. Your dad is excited to cuddle with Liz and me. Sleep good.

Love ya lots! – Ness

Monday

June 20, 2011

Jeff had left to run a few errands when I had come back that morning so I spent most of the day with Chris. He was working so hard at everything that he got worn out very easily. He slept a lot, and when he was awake between doctors and nurses, he was kept very busy. He was always thrilled when his dad came back into the room.

Jeff and I had headed home because Steph, Dana, and Liz were spending the night. It was a little easier leaving some nights because we knew Chris was in good hands, and he was doing so much better. When we walked out to the car, Jeff noticed that someone had run into our vehicle and left a pretty big dent on the driver's side. We both just looked at it wearily and proceeded to get into the car. The dent fix would have to wait until a later date. It just wasn't a priority for us then.

'BUILT TC TOUGH' POSTING – June 20th

I am so proud of my mom today. She has been with Chris all day. Simply holding his hand and hoping that she can take away just part of his pain. She is something else.

Amanda 'Benear' F

JOURNAL ENTRY – June 20th

Chris

Love ya – you made a not very happy face at me! I still love you! Keep fighting. You are so tough. Amazing! I am praying all the time. We miss you coming over and I actually miss you asking me for a meal! Ha, love you and get better soon and come over for that meal. You are that miracle! You are so amazing. God is watching over you every minute. You are blessed!

Laura

Chapter 14 – Writing Therapy for All

Tuesday – Day 16

June 21, 2011

Chris's cousins and friend had created an additional separate *'Facebook'* page so that other people could post to it for Chris to read later, and to keep people updated if they couldn't get to the hospital. It also replaced the blog web page that was previously created to keep people informed. The *'Facebook'* page was like having the journal online and it was called ***'FIGHTING WITH CHRIS/BUILT TC TOUGH'.***

I've always been a big talker, meaning my family says I can talk to anyone. I feel it never hurts to say hello to someone or strike up a conversation about any subject except politics. Some of those acquaintances have turned out, over the years, to be considered good friends. I was really not too surprised when a staff member who was in charge of the wing we were in on the fourth floor had brought me a three-ring binder. The binder was full of loose leaf paper and a couple of pens. She stated, "You are a very intriguing storyteller and easy to talk to, you might want to write a book sometime. If not, sometimes writing your thoughts down can be therapeutic." So, at quiet times we wrote. Our writings in the journal, my binder notes, and the **'FIGHTING WITH CHRIS/BUILT TC TOUGH'** *'Facebook'* page are very helpful with this phase of my writing therapy.

'FIGHTING WITH CHRIS/BUILT TC TOUGH'
POSTING – June 21st

Chris has been fighting for his life since his car accident, on the evening of June 5, 2011. The details that took place the evening of the 5th and the morning of the 6th are truly something you see in a movie, but to be respectful to the people close to him we are going to hold off on posting about the negatives. Instead, this blog will focus on the positives and all of the wonderful improvements he makes. Each passing day, he has continued to amaze us with his strength and perseverance. We thank Chris for not giving up and we thank God for remaining by his side during this difficult time.

Chris' Room A.M.

Dad, Chris, and I had a real emotional morning. Chris cried when his dad was telling him he was in the U of M hospital, and he had been in a car accident. Not the first time we had told him, but we think today he really understood what we were saying. Dad told him that we were all in this for the <u>long haul</u>.

Chris we are going to spend a lot more quality time together. I hope you can put up with your <u>mom's love</u>!

> Mom

I told Chris this morning that when he and I signed up together it was a lifetime commitment. I also told him that there were a lot of good times ahead to spend together and that we will plan things for the future. I think as sad as it was to hear Chris crying like he did this morning, it was a big step. It showed me that he realized it was me and that he realized he was hurt badly. He is trying to reach out to us the best he can at this point. I will cherish the day when my son and I can again talk to each other and make plans <u>TOGETHER</u>.

> Dad

'FIGHTING WITH CHRIS/BUILT TC TOUGH'
POSTING – June 21st

Today is a beautiful day!

What is 'just another Tuesday' to some and the first day of summer to others, is much more to the Benears, their family, and their friends.

<u>Today Chris Benear cried</u>. While we struggle with seeing Chris so vulnerable, we also shed tears of joy. This is truly a miracle. Not only do the tears tell us that he can see us and hear us, but they also tell us that he understands us. God is good!

Please don't be surprised if this post is deleted from the blog in the future. That only means that Chris found this post, read what it said, and then kicked my butt for telling everyone. Kissyfur, please know that you were not crying alone and you will never be <u>alone</u>. We will always be here for you.

So emotional for everyone involved today and not many extra words need to be written other than the three accounts above. Finally, we knew Chris was coming back to us and we were so excited and hopeful that he has finally turned a big corner. HE UNDERSTOOD US…HE WAS THERE. The morning really drained Chris and us so we had a pretty quiet rest of the day. Chris slept a lot and visitors took short visits, but everyone noticed he was doing better.

Emily

JOURNAL ENTRY – June 21st

Beaner

What up Homie! I've been busy for the last few days so I haven't been down to see U. I hear you're doing well though!!!

I hear you have your eyes open and are able to see a little. (Glad I wore my best shirt for my boy.)   That's a huge step from the last time I saw you. Well, keep being you and I'm sure you'll be outta here in no time.

Ryan M

JOURNAL ENTRY – June 21st

Hey Bud, need you back to softball. I need the batting title back. You looked good today, can't wait to talk.

Jake F

JOURNAL ENTRY – June 21st

Hey Chris ☺

You're looking good. Get all the rest you can. You are amazing. You're a hell of a guy. Keep up the good work and soon this will all be behind you! You just have a detour in the road. You have a wonderful support group. We all love you dearly. Prayers are out there!

Love – Kristi W

Chapter 15 – Writing Therapy Continues

Wednesday – Day 17

June 22, 2011

Chris seemed to be very active that day. I had taken time to walk a friend down to the elevator, took a quick phone call, and had come back to the room to see that Chris' legs were coming off the end of the bed. His head was way off the pillow and he had slid way down in the bed. There was no skull on the left side of Chris' head since it had been removed during surgery. I was always worried about him hitting his head on something. They had measured him for a helmet, but it had not arrived yet. When they removed the left side of Chris' skull, they had planned on re-attaching the skull at a later date when the swelling went down. They had noticed some bacteria growing on the removed portion so they had placed it in a freezer to protect it until they decided if it could be used safely for reattachment. The bacteria was growing because Chris had fallen into the swamp hole after his accident and the swamp water entered the hole created from the puncture wound.

Where was a nurse? I went and found the nurse. She had come directly in and couldn't believe how far he had wiggled. She was excited at how he was moving so she ordered a bigger bed. She was excited, I was scared.

JOURNAL ENTRY – June 22nd

Beans

Oh my god dude you're doing <u>awesome</u>! It's Wednesday and I haven't seen you since Friday, what an improvement. Minus you not being able to talk back to me, you're doing great. It was really nice talking to you and knowing that you can hear and see me and know that it's me. I was gonna come down this past Sunday, but Howard and I had to do two pig roasts with five pigs so it was late by the time we were done. But, I made it today and will be back by Saturday for sure at the latest. Ma B is making dinner for me to bring up to everyone so sure it'll be some good shit.

We brought a big group up here to see you today. Me, Wigg, Muff, Tommy, Kiel, Nek, and even your boy Squado is here. I think I should stop writing in this thing so much because everyone keeps making fun of me for it LOL. Well I guess I can handle it.

I just want you to know that I love you brother, and I'm thinking about you non-stop. I can't wait till you get outta this place <u>MAN</u>. I have some good plans in store for US LOL! Take care man.

Love ya Beans – Bains

JOURNAL ENTRY – 9:22 p.m. June 22nd

Bean

You had quite the crew in here tonight. You're a local Superhero. You tried to crawl out of bed today – crazy kid. The story made me smile. You are just so dang determined to be better and it's working well. The amount of progress you make each day is incredible and only you could make it possible.

Your nurses love you. Stephanie, one of your night nurses, even added me on *'Facebook'* so I could keep her posted. My ♡ for U of M increases every day.

We have one hell of a plan for a fundraiser for you. You'd be so impressed. Ben N brought in the very first shirt made for you. They look so great. I can't wait for there to be hundreds of them around town. Like I said, you're our local Superhero.

I am so glad you are starting to recognize us. I know it must be hard for you not to be able to communicate with us, but soon Bean, soon.

Tomorrow is Amanda's b-day so be sure to give her an extra-special b-day squeeze. ☺

Well – I hope you rest well tonight. I'll be sure not to bug you during my shift and try to let you sleep. See ya in the a.m.

Always – ♡ Ness

Chapter 16 – Big Sis' Birthday

Thursday – Day 18

June 23, 2011

Chris had a very restless night. We now know that he understands more and more and the frustration level must be so high for him. Chris was such a hard worker, and just like his dad it seems they are both happier the busier they are. I'm sure he is worried about his recovery process, his job, his lawn mowing business, his family, his home, and what his life is going to look like post-accident. It's extremely hard as a parent when you can't ease your child's worries and take away their pain.

When I came back into Chris' room, his two nurses had him sitting up in a recliner – <u>WOW</u>.

JOURNAL ENTRY – 8:25 a.m. June 23th

Good morning Chris! You had a very active night last night; you kept us girls busy! We wouldn't want it any other way. I know this is frustrating for you, but I also know that you will never stop fighting and you will not let anything beat you. I am very proud of you, your strength, your determination, and your will, especially your will to get the tracheotomy tube out of your throat.☺ I know you will be back to us very soon and I am looking forward to hearing all about your journey first hand.

Love you – Liz

'FIGHTING WITH CHRIS/BUILT TC TOUGH' POSTING – June 23th

Today Chris' oldest sister, Amanda, was not only able to celebrate her birthday with Chris, but she also received an unexpected birthday gift from Chris.

Today Chris smiled and was able to sit in a chair!

Last night Chris was very active; constantly moving and trying to get up. When the doctors heard and saw what the nurses and family members were seeing, they decided to let Chris have his way and try to get him out of bed. (Might as well, he's not going to stop until he gets what he wants.) In no time at all, he was sitting up in the recliner chair in his room all by himself.

At that time, Amanda had no idea what was going on and her only birthday request was for Chris to squeeze her hand. Boy was she in for a treat. When she arrived, not only did he squeeze her hand, he was out of bed and he smiled at her for the first time since the accident!

Everyone was surprised that Chris lasted around four hours sitting up in the chair. It has been nineteen days since his accident and seeing his determination to get better gave us all new energy and hope for the future.

Team Benear

JOURNAL ENTRY – 6:30 p.m. June 23th

Hey Chris!

Your Aunt Paula and I just got back to the 'NICU Inn' – the family waiting room we've taken over. There was some very good news from your doctor. She wanted you to straighten your left fingers, wiggle your left toes, and bend your left knee and you did it all! All she could say was, "WOW"! You continue to amaze everyone Chris. You are looking better every day and you continue to improve, impressing everyone. I spent some time with you after the doctor left and you looked right at me. I know you are aware of your surroundings because you move your eyes toward whoever is talking. We are all so proud of you and we love you so much!

Fighting with Chris! – Jessica B

JOURNAL ENTRY – 9:45 p.m. June 23th

Best Birthday Gift Ever!

The last couple of days I have been back in Grand Rapids with the kids, missing you <u>bad</u>. I was so excited to see you on my birthday and all I wanted was a small hand squeeze from you. Not only did I get a squeeze, but I even got a <u>smile.</u> ☺ It was absolutely <u>perfect</u>.

Keep fighting Chris and I miss you. ☺

     Amanda

Chapter 17 – Progress

Friday – Day 19

June 24, 2011

Things had seemed to be moving along. Chris had made great progress the day before with sitting up in the recliner for almost four hours. Then on June 24th, they disconnected his ventilator.

On the 24th, Chris also took his first question quiz, and he passed!!! They asked him to wiggle his left toes when she said the right answer to the question.

What is your name?

    a.   Ed (no movement)

    b.   Rick (no movement)

    c.   Chris (The left foot started moving!)

What year is it?

    a. 2055 (no movement)

    b. 1994 (no movement)

    c. 2005 (no movement)

    d. 2011 (More left foot movement!)

Where are you?

    a. At home (no movement)

    b. At the grocery store (no movement)

    c. At the hospital

       (Lots of left foot movement and an ugly face too!)

Are you cold? (no movement)

Are you warm? (no movement)

Are you comfortable? (no movement)

Are you uncomfortable? (His whole left leg started moving!)

Then they asked him to move his right foot. He tried really hard, but wasn't able to move it. The facial expression he was making told us that he was doing everything he could, but it just wasn't happening.

You could see that he was exhausted. To celebrate getting all the questions right, the nurse had asked Chris to give Emily a high-five. With an elbow on the bed, he lifted his left hand and hit her hand. The nurse asked Chris to go a little higher; he tried, but really struggled.

The nurse raised his hand a little higher and then released it. Chris was able to keep it raised by himself for a couple of seconds…what a day!

I left the hospital to go to the court house. Jeff and I had applied to be Chris' guardians shortly after the accident so we could handle all of his legal affairs. The court had sent a representative for Chris to make sure no one was taking advantage of him or his assets. The gentleman had come in a week ago or so and asked me if it would be okay for him to interview Chris on behalf of the court. I told him absolutely, and if he could get Chris to talk I would buy him a steak dinner. After an awkward look from him, I escorted him to Chris' room. After spending some time with Chris, he had come back and told me good luck with your son, and said that he would see me in court soon.

I had very little knowledge of court proceedings, so thankfully through my daughter's work place I had a great lawyer named Laura. She met me at the court and explained what was about to happen. When our case was called, we proceeded to the front table and I sat down.

Chris' advocate had spoken on his behalf, and before I knew it, his part was over. My lawyer had made sure Jeff and I were put on as equals so either one of us could sign, then the judge wished me and Chris good luck, and we were done. Something that had been so scary and made me nervous going in was handled so efficiently that it put me at ease. I don't remember everything Chris' advocate mentioned, probably because I was emotional and had a very hard time keeping it together. I do remember him stating that Chris' Mom and Dad were very supportive and loving parents that had their son's best interests at heart. He had taken that away from our short encounter at the hospital and it made me feel so peaceful. During a time in my life where I hadn't felt much like anything was going the way I wanted or the way things should be going, a total stranger got it! He just got it!

JOURNAL ENTRY – June 24th

Chris

We are still praying and thinking of you always! Each night if I stir in the middle of the night I pray all over again. I figure God is probably less busy then, and I will get more one on one attention! ☺

Love – Sarah P

'FIGHTING WITH CHRIS/BUILT TC TOUGH' POSTING – June 24th

Hey Chris,

I decided to take a turn with the slumber party! I'm having a great time! Thanks for inviting me! Your mom, dad, and Emily are all here. Everyone's sleeping like a baby, including you! I thank God for all he's done! We pray for you to keep fighting. I know you will!! Your mom and dad enjoyed the hugs today!

Cynda M. B

Chapter 18 – Post Surgery Days

Saturday – Day 20

June 25, 2011

I had entered Chris' room that evening after returning to the hospital from running errands. Talk about being a <u>LITTLE JEALOUS</u>. Dad had said he had received a hug from Chris earlier that day. It was kind of like when you have a new baby and you want their first word to be momma; I'd been aching for a hug. After I had entered Chris' room, I walked over to his bedside and started talking to him. Chris raised his left arm around my shoulder and pulled me towards him. WOW, I had gotten my <u>hug</u>!

As the day wore on, Chris had started to cough. I asked him if he wanted them to suction him out, he winked once for yes. After the Nurse left the room, Chris shut his eyes. All was quiet except for the hum of the television.

Chris had always had good hearing. Since the accident, his hearing had become more acute. We had the Tigers' game on with really low volume, but he seemed to be hearing it just fine. <u>A</u> <u>Really</u> <u>Good</u> <u>Day</u> <u>Thanks!</u>

JOURNAL ENTRY – June 25th

I was in the room with Chris. Pam, his nurse today, was asking him to help lift his legs so she could change his bandages. He did everything he was told. Then she asked him to hold the hoist cord for her and he reached up and held it two times.

Chris acted as if he was in some pain so I got down close to his face with mine and said "I wish I knew what I could do to make you feel better." He put his arm around me and pulled me in tight. Best <u>HUG</u> I have gotten in a long time, <u>AWESOME</u>.

Today was a good day! – Dad

'FIGHTING WITH CHRIS/BUILT TC TOUGH'
POSTING – June 25th

Hi Chris,

Wish you and your family better news to come!! There are a lot of angels out there rooting for you ☺ so enjoy and please get well. I can't stand not talking to ya! I know it's gonna take time and I know you of all people can do this! Just keep your hopes, strength, and head up please!!! We all love you so much☺. Be safe, sweet dreams, and see you soon!!

Love Kristi W

Left: Chris
Howell Melon Prince (1985)

Above: Chris & Jeff (1987)

Left: Chris and Grandma Jean (2001)

Below: Chris and Jeff (2010)

Below: Chris and Jack
First buck using crossbow since
accident (2014)

Above: Chris
surrounded by
hospital therapy staff
(2011)

Below: Left to right —
Jeff, Jack & Chris
fishing (2013)

Right: Dave, Chris, and Liz at a Tigers baseball game (2019)

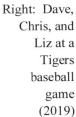

Above: Alex, Stephanie, Justin and Amanda at a fundraiser for Chris (2011)

Right: Amanda, Stephanie, and Chris (2018)

Above: Chris and
cousin Emily (1998)

Right: Chris and
Vanessa (2009)

Above: Chris and
Uncle John (2013)

Above: Chris and Dave at a friend's
wedding (2013)

Left: Chris (2015)

Chapter 19 – The Helmet

Sunday – Day 21

June 26, 2011

Earlier that day Chris had been fitted for a helmet. The helmet was to protect his head due to there being no skull and only skin covering his left side. He hated it!!! Justin had spent the night so he and Jeff had the job of making Chris wear his helmet that first day.

Since Chris had a good nights sleep and had been given the new helmet they thought he was ready for some physical therapy. Chris seemed to be excited and anxious. With the help of Jeff, the therapist had started working with Chris' legs. The therapist would work with his right leg and Jeff would do the same with his left. Then Jeff became a cheerleader as the therapist started to work with Chris' left arm. While she had tried to get Chris to raise his arm up as high as he could for ten repetitions (reps), after three reps it had seemed that he hadn't been interested enough to finish. Then Jeff tried to encourage him by asking him to give some high fives to finish up his reps. He finished his seven reps with his left hand by raising his arm up as high as he could. The therapist had been overjoyed that Chris had accomplished this, and asked Chris to give her a high five. Chris opened his hand up to really make the high five count. Chris knowing that a true high five only happens with an open hand was <u>huge</u>. Everyone let out a loud celebratory cheer. The left side of his beautiful smile moved just enough for us to know that Chris was celebrating inside too. ☺

After how well Chris had done in his workout, the therapist decided to give him another opportunity to sit in the recliner chair next to his bed. Jeff and the therapist had Chris in the chair in no time. It was great seeing him sit up and stretch his long frame out to work out his left leg. He looked so comfortable. Once his right leg was reclining he put his left leg on the ground. It seemed to make him happy to have his foot down on the floor. Justin had been sitting right by Chris and had been willing to help him lift his leg back up, but Chris lifted his leg and he made it look easy and effortless. He was so determined to do as much as possible on his own.

Chris had seemed to love the chair and his workout, but he was not excited about having to wear the helmet when he was sitting up. When he thought Jeff and Justin were distracted, he would grab for the snap to release his helmet, but the guys would stop him before he could get it unsnapped. Then Chris tried another tactic. He acted like there was something wrong with the heart rate monitor on his left finger. Jeff, who was always ready to help Chris in any way he could, jumped up and proceeded to the chair. He was in the process of moving the clamp from Chris' left finger to place it on his right finger and was focusing on adjusting the monitor clamp correctly when Chris again reached up to unsnap and remove his helmet. Each time he thought Jeff was distracted, Chris would try to unsnap his helmet, but luckily Justin was there paying attention and Chris' plan to take the helmet off was foiled. Chris had continued to try to sneak one past his old man, but the tag team of Justin and Jeff was too much for Chris to overcome. Justin and Jeff had won another round.

JOURNAL ENTRY – June 26th

Hey Bean –

Kiel and I are back to visit. I brought you a communication board today. I'm hoping maybe it'll help you talk to us to ease some of the frustration.

We've got quite the t-shirt and wrist band wait list going. I can't believe how many supporters you have. The auction is getting out of control – you'd be so impressed. I can't wait for you to get better so you can see everyone in your shirts and wearing your wristbands.

Well I gotta get into that room of yours to see your big eyes. I'll see you tomorrow. I'm having a sleepover with your mom and dad. Suey and Jeffro are coming tomorrow too. They're bringing dinner.

Lots of Love xoxo – Vanessa

JOURNAL ENTRY – June 26th

Hey Brother –

You look really good today. I was just visiting with you and you patted me on the back. It felt so good to have your hand sitting there. I am so proud of everything you have been doing. And I heard you gave Dad a <u>hug</u>. He loved it!! You are so impressive little brother. I think you learned it <u>all</u> from me. ☺

Love you – Amanda

'FIGHTING WITH CHRIS/BUILT TC TOUGH'
POSTING – June 26th

Good morning Chris. I have a voicemail on my phone from you from a few weeks ago. When I was listening to my messages the other day I heard it again. "Nessieeeeeee—it's the Beaner…" At first it was so hard, but now (this might seem weird) I try to listen to it once a day. I love hearing your voice and know that you'll be able to talk to us again soon. I'm coming tonight to have a sleepover at the 'Resort' with your mom and dad. Yesterday you even gave hugs. WOW – that's amazing Chris. You really made your mom's day. I'm thinking we'll practice with the communication board and maybe even get some sleep this time.

Lots of love xoxo – Vanessa M

'FIGHTING WITH CHRIS/BUILT TC TOUGH'
POSTING – June 26th

Hi Chris, I have been reading the posts on here every day. Sometimes I look at them several times a day. It has just amazed me – the amount of love and support that people have given you and your family. I mean I can see why. I know your mom Mary and she is an AMAZING woman! I know you through her and when you have taken care of my mom, Lana, and brought campfire wood out to her summer home in Durand. She always talked about Chris and what a nice guy you are. I have struggled at what to say to you and your family. I went to see you about a week ago and was again amazed by the love and support. People everywhere just waiting for you to wake up. They have set up the "Beaner Inn" and people are there around the clock. I know you must be overwhelmed by all the attention, I sure was. I went with my mom and your mom to see you, and I gotta tell you, even not knowing you very well, it broke my heart to see that guy who had dropped off wood for us not long ago being there in that hospital bed! Here I was trying to be there for your mom and instead she is taking care of me! I just want you to know that I think of you and your family ALL the time and KNOW you are a FIGHTER. Your story has restored some faith that had been lost in my own life. Your family's love and all the people that have been there for you have restored some things in my life that had been forgotten. All that I can say is keep fighting and know that I will fight and pray with all of you. See you soon.

Love – Cheryl O

'FIGHTING WITH CHRIS/BUILT TC TOUGH'
POSTING – June 26th

Hey Chris,

I wish I could be right next to you, letting you know I love you. Day to day things seem meaningless compared with the work you are doing now. Mom and I were saying it was hard to believe that the whole world did not stop when ours did three weeks ago. Anyway, I just wanted you to know not an hour passes that I don't think of you and thank God for you!

    Jamie F

'FIGHTING WITH CHRIS/BUILT TC TOUGH'
POSTING – June 26th

Chris,

I hear you're just blowing those doctors away with your speedy recovery. When you're able, maybe you can fill them in and tell them how important faith, hope and love are in the healing process! God and prayers have been with you every step of the way. Remember, that which doesn't kill us only makes us stronger. You're a strong man!

    God bless! – Ma Bain

Chapter 20 – Taking Turns

Monday – Day 22

June 27, 2011

Jeff went back to work on June 27th after taking three weeks off. We had decided he would try to work Mondays, Wednesdays, and Fridays. He would spend Tuesdays and Thursdays at the hospital and I would go home. He had gone home that night to sleep and would be back on June 28th at 6:00 p.m.

Chris had a really rough night and day. It was like he was upset that his dad wasn't there. I had a real hard time quieting him down. He kept watching the door and was just out of sorts all day. I told Chris that Dad would be down later and that he went to work.

Jeff came in around 6:30 p.m., went right to Chris, and laid his head next to Chris' head on the bed. Chris raised his left arm up around his dad to give him a hug and then closed his eyes.

The bond between Chris and his dad has always been so <u>special</u>. When you hear people say their dad is their best friend, you might smirk a little, but believe me I will never ever question that about anyone again because I have witnessed that bond first hand.

I left Chris in great hands and headed home. After driving the thirty five minutes home, I sat out on my swing and returned a few phone calls, then went inside. It was so quiet and empty. I felt terrible being there by myself. Jeff and I usually came home together when 'Team Benear' took over for us to give us a break. We both felt empty when we left Chris at the hospital. We knew we had come a long way, but the road was going to be even longer and we needed to keep ourselves together. The road never seemed as difficult when we were together. Coming home alone was extremely hard. I had to take my mind off that feeling. I wrote out some bills then decided to call it an evening and fell asleep on the couch. The bed, without Jeff there with me, was not an option.

JOURNAL ENTRY – June 27th

Good Morning Christopher!

Well it's Monday morning and I slept until ten! Of course, that's only about five hours, so I guess I don't feel so bad about it. I stayed here at the 'NICU Inn' last night with Jodi, Liz, and Steph.

I got to spend a couple of hours with you in the middle of the night. I have been saying the last couple of days that I wanted you to be awake when I see you. All these people have good stories of you squeezing their hands and all sorts of other things to communicate. It seems that when I see you, you are almost always resting. Well, be careful what you ask for!

You were awake for almost the whole time I was with you. (Two to four a.m. - you really need to get your nights and days straightened out.) Boy, were you feisty! You started by giving me a hug! I'm pretty sure you were trying to get me to help you escape, but I'm going to call it a hug until you say otherwise. You also squeezed my hand and gave me a high five. You touched my hand when I asked you to, and you swatted it away from your face when I was trying to keep you from grinding your teeth. You kept trying to escape all night.

We know you don't want to be here, and before you know it you'll be home. In the meantime, you always have two or three people here to be with you. You're making such great progress and it won't be long until all of this is just a story you tell to impress everyone and show them how tough you are! Keep up the good work.

Love you – Stacy

'FIGHTING WITH CHRIS/BUILT TC TOUGH'
POSTING – June 27th

This morning Chris was agitated, as he has been over the last week, which we all expect considering his determination and his current limitations. As we, I was in the room with his sister

Stephanie, had tried to comfort him and assure him we were there for him, another miracle occurred. Chris was grabbing for my arm trying to pull himself up to get out of bed when his sister Steph calmly asked him if he could give me a hug.

He reached to pull himself up. I turned into him and he reached to pull me close. By putting his left hand around my back, he pulled me down to his chest. That had to be the best feeling I have felt thus far in my life! I lay on his chest for what seemed like an eternity, but was maybe only a minute. I have never felt more love and admiration from a hug than I did this morning. I am hoping he felt the same way I did including that sense of security that we all feel when we are hugged. In that moment, with that hug, the security I have always felt in a hug was amplified and I only pray that Chris was able to feel that same amplified sense of security and love. Chris knows I am not one to cry, but I will tell you the tears welled up in my eyes as I lay on his chest.

Chris when you read this, I just wanted you to know you brought me to tears. Hopefully, that helps you understand the love and security that has been bestowed upon you and our entire family over the last three weeks.

There is not a more loving family or group of friends than the ones we are blessed to have. Thank you to my family for never breaking, and thank you to our friends for always letting us be exactly who we are and loving us by choice. They always say you don't get to pick your family. If I had it my way, we would all be family! Love you all! Have a great day in honor of each of Chris' great days, past, present, and future!

Liz B

'FIGHTING WITH CHRIS/BUILT TC TOUGH' POSTING – June 27th

Today marks three weeks. It is hard Chris. I miss you so much. I think about you constantly, and want you to know how amazingly proud I am to tell everyone that you are my little brother. You have touched so many people. I always knew that your heart was huge and your personality magnetic. But over the past three weeks it has been truly remarkable to see all of the people that love you come together to fight with you and help you overcome this difficult life obstacle. We will get through this. And when we do, I am going to take a long time telling you how much I love you. You are my hero!

Love, love, love – Amanda 'Benear' F

'FIGHTING WITH CHRIS/BUILT TC TOUGH' POSTING – June 27th

Chris sure is determined. Oh and from the sounds of it, Chris is doing everything he can to continue to tell us how he truly feels. Mary, Chris' mom, was in with him today and when he started moving around she asked him to give her a high five when she hit on the right answer for his restlessness:

Are you cold? (no movement)

Are you hot? (no movement)

Are you in pain? (no movement)

Are you uncomfortable? (no movement)

Do you just want me to shut-up and leave you alone? (His left hand gave her the hardest high five he possibly could!)

Lesson of the day; don't ask a question unless you are prepared to hear the answer. (In this case, Mary was prepared, completely understood, and simply wanted to do whatever it took to help her son.)

Vanessa

Chapter 21 – Milestones

Tuesday – Day 23

June 28, 2011

Chris left the ICU on June 28th after twenty-one days. We had mixed emotions. Chris had been getting better every day, which was great, but leaving the nurses and staff who we considered part of our extended family was difficult. We would miss them so much. They held our hands, gave us encouragement, and shared some laughs and a lot of tears. Some people might say that hospital staff does not care, that their patients are just another number. Maybe it was our hospitality room which had been kept stocked with treats, Chris' story of survival (Rambo), or maybe we were just friendly people that they enjoyed spending time with in their continual days of difficult work situations. I believe it was because they really cared about their patients. So we moved to the step down unit with mixed emotions.

We continued to make sure Chris' vitals stayed strong and he was getting everything he needed medically. From what everyone said, time was what he needed the most - time for his brain to heal.

JOURNAL ENTRY – 9:40 a.m. June 28th

Kissyfur --

Hey There! I can't believe it, but I totally forgot to write in here yesterday. We had another sleep over. You were quite feisty between one and five a.m. again. I can't wait until you can tell us what's wrong!

Everyone is lovin' your hugs. I got several last night, which made me smile. I played you some music from your CD last night. I think you enjoyed <u>it</u>.

♡ ya lots – Nessie

Wednesday - Day 24

June 29, 2011

We stayed two nights on the floor we called the step down ward. Our next stop would be the Rehabilitation division on 6A.

The step down ward seemed to be a little under-staffed compared to the ICU. We continued to have one of us in Chris' room at all times. I thought he was more alert and understood things that were going on a little more, a mother's hope?

The doctors had been questioning whether or not Chris was ready for rehabilitation (rehab) this early in his recovery process. They wanted to run more tests and get good results back before they cleared him for the strain rehab would put on his body and brain. Well, they asked for it and Chris gave it to them. Chris' tests had come back 'all good' so the doctors approved rehab. He would be moved the next day.

JOURNAL ENTRY – June 29th

Beans!

What's up BRUTHA! You amaze me every time I come down. This time you just got your new room and still managed to keep a hot nurse.

I don't know how you do it, but the good looking women seem to follow you around here…

But anyway, I'm amazed at how good you're lookin'. I think all the hard work everyone has been putting you through is paying off. Well, keep it up Beans, you're my IDOL.

Ryan M

Thursday – Day 25

June 30, 2011

Chris was moved to the rehabilitation unit on 6A at around 1:30 on June 30th. That day had started out really rough. Somehow Chris was put in a smaller bed. Because Chris had no bone on the left side of his skull, I remember the doctor saying to keep him in the bed that was very roomy and keep his helmet on. I lost it with the head nurse when she told me she had made the decision to use the smaller bed because the smaller bed would be a better fit for his new room.

Chris was taken down for his very first physical therapy (PT) session at 3:30. Chris, with the help of a lot of other people, stood for the first time since June 5th. Dad thought he had a really good look on his face. Standing massively wore him out. Starting Friday, July 1st, he was to go to physical therapy twice a day. They had a lift in his room that they used to get Chris in and out of bed and onto transport each time he was scheduled to go to physical therapy.

When we arrived back in Chris' room after that first PT session, his bed had pads on all parts of each railing on both sides of the bed. I felt much better and later that week the head nurse and I finally smiled at each other. She assured me that she and the head doctor had agreed that this would work.

Friday – Day 26

July 1, 2011

Friday was a work day for Jeff so my sister Betty escorted Chris to his first session of PT that day. I did some catch up work then escorted Chris to his second PT session. The main strategy, at that point, was to get Chris to try to hold his head up strong. They told Chris that if he would hold his head up strong, then they would allow him to try to take a step. Chris had taken his left foot and tried to step forward. He surprised them with his 'all in' attitude.

Chris had always given everything 110 percent. Hunting – playing cards – sports – his business – whatever he was doing, he gave it everything and then some. I knew he could tell his recovery road would be a long haul, but he had been ready to see some results in the first steps he took. His communication skills were still very primitive, but he seemed to make them understand that he wanted it really badly.

Chris also started speech therapy (SP) and occupational therapy (OT). His work load was hard and so draining on him. Some days they had barely gotten him back in bed just to get him out again for something else.

Chris seemed to be a lot less restless. With the brain injury he would tire very easily. Every chance he got, he closed his eyes.

JOURNAL ENTRY – July 1st

Hi Chris,

I haven't been here in a couple of days and I couldn't believe how far you've come. You look like Chris again.

You are doing great. You're amazing to everyone, everyday there's so much progress! I can't wait to talk to you. Prayers are being said for you day and night.

Love you – Linda B

JOURNAL ENTRY – July 1st

Chris

Hey Big Fella! I just wanted to let you know you did it again. You have amazed me once again! Every time I come down you show so much progress it's amazing! It inspires me to come down often to be a witness to your hard work. So keep it up and until next time you will stay in my thoughts and <u>PRAYERS</u>.

Ryan M

Saturday – Day 27

July 2, 2011

Chris was in intensive rehab from 9:00 a.m. to 3:00 p.m. every day. The doctors had requested quiet time during the day in between rehab sessions. They had wanted Chris to have no extra stimulation so he could focus on his therapy. They had wanted as much quiet time for him during the day as possible, but felt that visitors from 6:00 p.m. to 8:00 p.m. would keep his spirits up…if he was sleeping we were to leave him be.

The doctors had explained to us that there were eight steps Chris would go through on the Rancho Los Amigos Levels of Cognitive Functioning scale (Rancho). Rancho was about the art and science of medical rehabilitation. Chris was at the third level with a lot of hard work ahead of him.

Chris was very tired a lot during the day, but he seemed to be able to concentrate when he had rehab which just showed his determination and will to get back to his old self.

Those first few all day rehab days were very hard on him…and his mom. I had struggled watching my son, who is one of the strongest people I know, being so vulnerable and tiring so easily. Speech therapy, physical therapy, occupational therapy, doctors, tests, and social workers had become very overwhelming for me and I was just a bystander. Chris' perseverance and strong will to get better and go home was so inspiring to me and all of 'Team Benear'.

Unlike some car accidents where there is a closed head injury, Chris' accident had resulted in a tree limb penetrating the left side of his brain. In the earlier days, the doctors had made us fully aware of the small chance of Chris surviving, but they had also let us know what the left side of the brain controlled if he did survive:

Left Side –

- Understanding and use of language (listening, reading, speaking, and writing).
- Memory for spoken and written messages.
- Detailed analysis of information.
- Controls the right side of the body.

So with communication and language being a big concern over the last weeks, Chris had been making great strides in understanding what was being said to him, and understood most written words the therapists were using. He had also progressed in being able to move his left side, progressing faster than the doctors had hoped for. <u>Miracle.</u>

Monday – Fourth of July – Day 29

July 4, 2011

JOURNAL ENTRY – July 4th

Hey Chris!!

Happy Fourth of July!! I was so excited to see you today. I had been hearing all about your progress. I had to come see for myself. I felt so honored that you had saved a hug for me. I can't believe how great you are looking. You are amazing and such a source of pride for our family.

I love you – Jamie

JOURNAL ENTRY – July 4th

Hi Chris!

Happy Fourth of July! Thanks for the hug today! It was great to see you, it had been two days and you looked better today – amazing! You will owe me for the back rubs I gave you. Okay, well maybe I will give you a pass and consider those freebies. ☺ Your lips were a little chapped so I gave you some Carmex!

Now I know what to bring you next time I come down. Keep workin' hard.

Love you lots – Liz

P.S. You gave the thumbs down today…we will keep it a secret as to what the question was. ☺ See you soon!

Tuesday – Day 30

July 5, 2011

JOURNAL ENTRY – July 5th

Chris - ☺

<u>Wow</u>!! That is all I could say – it has been two weeks since I saw you last and WOW!! Can't wait to see you next time. Keep up the <u>hard</u> <u>work</u>!!

Love – Cheryl O

'FIGHTING WITH CHRIS/BUILT TC TOUGH'
POSTING – July 5th

Today in therapy, a nurse asked Chris to remove pegs from a peg board and put them in a bucket. After just staring at the nurse for a minute, the nurse explained again that she needed all of the blue and yellow pegs off the board and into the bucket. After encouraging him two or three more times, Chris reached up, removed one of the blue pegs and put it in the bucket. The nurse congratulated Chris and went on to push him to remove a yellow peg from the board and to put it in the bucket. After additional encouragement, Chris did as she requested. The nurse asked him repeatedly to remove a few more pegs before having to move on to a different patient, saying "keep working on getting those pegs off the board for me Chris." Once the nurse stepped away, Chris took a break from touching the pegs…not wanting to do any of this in the first place. After the nurse was away for a bit without Chris making a move, Jeff (Chris' dad) stepped up to the front of Chris and told Chris that he needed to keep removing the pegs for the nurse. Being the loving father that Jeff is, Jeff even offered to help him out a bit.

At about that time, Jeff and Chris made eye contact and Chris gave him a rather annoyed look. Chris then proceeded to remove a number of pegs all at the same time with only his left hand, dropping them all in the bucket at once. All Jeff could do was smile.

As frustrating as it is for Chris, we are thankful for his continued hard work through this difficult time. All of these small steps may be easy to achieve for most, but to make sure that Chris continues to progress at the right rate, these are steps that he needs to take.

Team Benear

Saturday

July 9, 2011

'FIGHTING WITH CHRIS/BUILT TC TOUGH'
POSTING – July 9ᵗʰ

A note from Chris' family:

As many of you know, Chris has made great progress in the last few weeks. He is really working hard, and proving to us every day that he is quite the fighter. His will is awe inspiring!

My parents wanted to let everyone know that visiting hours are no longer limited from 6:00 p.m. to 8:00 p.m. During the week, Chris is in and out of rehab from 9:00 a.m. to 3:00 p.m.ish with an hour long break during lunch (usually). If you would like to come during the week, you can either come during lunch or after 4:00 p.m. On the weekend, Chris generally does not have rehab, so please come whenever you would like. Our family loves the company.

One final note: There are really no words, but I will try anyway...Thank you! Thank you so much to the people who surround us with love, kindness, and support. The compassion you have shared with us during this time has been amazing. One day, we will thank each and every one of you individually. But for now, please know that we are truly moved.

<u>Love</u> the Benear Family –

Jeff, Mary, Amanda, Stephanie, and CHRIS!!!!

'FIGHTING WITH CHRIS/BUILT TC TOUGH'
POSTING – July 9th

Today in physical therapy the nurse was asking Chris to sit up as straight as he could. His sister Stephanie was by his side the whole time and was doing her best to encourage him.

With Stephanie at about five feet eight inches and Chris at six feet four inches, Stephanie started reminding Chris that he should be sitting taller than she is sitting. Reminding him over and over again, "you're taller than me, so you should be taller than me sitting up", and "come on buddy, I'm still taller than you." Well, after about four more of those kinds of statements, Chris reached over and (without Stephanie being ready for it) gave Stephanie such a hard shove she went flying off the mat...boy did the doctors love seeing that!

Everyone involved couldn't stop laughing (and Stephanie knew to back off a bit more). Anyone who knows Chris has seen him trying to get his sisters away from him in the past and knows that he always wins.

Got to love siblings.

Team Benear

Sunday

July 10, 2011

'FIGHTING WITH CHRIS/BUILT TC TOUGH' POSTING – July 10th

Today Chris played his first hand of Spades. It was Mary (his mom) and David (his uncle) against Chris and Betty (his aunt). Chris had no problem bidding the right amount of tricks and no problem picking the right card. His only downfall was his partner Betty. Betty bid too much and got set causing them to lose the game…she sure does owe Chris one!

Team Benear

'FIGHTING WITH CHRIS/BUILT TC TOUGH' POSTING – July 10th

Chris had some family friends, Nate and his wife Laura, in to visit today. When it was time to say goodbye, Stephanie (his sister) suggested Chris give Laura a hug because she hadn't felt the wonderful love filled squeeze that Chris has been giving to some of his visitors lately. With that, Chris reached out, wrapped his left arm around Laura and pulled her in real tight. Unlike most hugs that seemed to only last seconds, Chris held onto Laura a bit longer.

Nate, standing on the other side of Chris, saw the opportunity and took it saying, "Hey man, my hugs have never lasted that long.

Remember now, that's my wife you're hugging...what's going on here?!? Better yet, by the looks of it, Stephanie and I might need to step out of the room and give the two of you some alone time." About half way through Nate saying all of this, Laura and Stephanie started cracking up. By the time Nate was done, Chris' smile was from ear to ear. **This is the first time Chris' smile has extended to the right side!**

Nate and Laura, I can only imagine the two of you still have smiles on your faces too...thanks so much for being so great!

Team Benear

Chapter 22 – Staying Strong

July 16, 2011 through July 24, 2011

A few days ago Chris' trach was reduced from an eight to a six. The doctors had explained to us that most people cannot talk when their trach is at a six, but some men push through to make some noises. This morning when Jeff had gone into Chris' room, Chris said, "good morning" to his dad. It might not have been completely clear, but to his dad it was crystal clear. Another Miracle!

Every time Chris had accomplished something new or had done it for the first time since his accident, it gave us a great sense of hope and proved to us that he was getting stronger and here to stay.

'FIGHTING WITH CHRIS/BUILT TC TOUGH'
POSTING – July 16th

I just wanted to say how grateful I am that I had the opportunity to meet such a strong-willed man and all of the support that comes with him. What a great support system…I have never seen anything like it. I am sad that I only got to meet all of these great people under such devastating circumstances, but in the end it seems that this has only brought an unthinkably close family even closer. I think about Chris daily and I love reading about his accomplishments.

Thank you for keeping the world informed on his progress. It was a true pleasure to be his nurse. His story has opened my eyes and helped me realize that what sounds unthinkable is far from impossible.

Stephanie W

'FIGHTING WITH CHRIS/BUILT TC TOUGH'
POSTING – July 19th

Chris had a great day in therapy today and continues to stay strong through the difficult portion of his day. No matter how painful it is (or how annoying we are), Chris is putting 110% toward getting better. Today it was also mentioned that he seems to have moved into the fourth level of Rancho's eight levels. It may be a difficult level, but if anyone can make it through it is Chris. With his family by his side, prayers and positive thoughts from you, and God's help he'll be on his way to the fifth level in no time at all.

Another important note to make pertains to the wonderful people surrounding him each and every day. With Chris not able to stick up for himself as much as he would like to, his mother, father, sisters, brother-in law, soon to be brother-in-law, additional family, and friends have stepped right in to make sure he is receiving nothing but the best. Whether it's taking him to therapy or just making sure he has plenty of ice chips (Boy does he love his ice chips!), he has had someone with him 24 hours a day since the morning of June 6th. The love and dedication of the people around him is priceless.

Team Benear

'FIGHTING WITH CHRIS/BUILT TC TOUGH' POSTING – July 21th

He'll be keeping an eye on his dad from now on.

Today Chris played Euchre with his dad, mom, and a hospital nurse. After having a rough go at Spades (due to his partner being set), Chris got to pick his partner for the game. When his mom asked him if he wanted to be partners with his dad, he shook his head no and pointed at his mom. Anyone who knows the Benear family knows that Chris and his mom are the die-hard card players of the bunch…good pick Chris!

Once the teams were determined, Chris was given the cards to deal out. As Chris was dealing, his dad didn't think he was paying much attention, so he picked up two of Chris' cards and took a look at them. Big Mistake! Chris instantly stopped dealing and gave his dad a nasty face. Ha! His dad apologized and the card game continued, but Chris kept a close eye on his dad for the rest of the game. Chris and his mom <u>WON</u>.

Team Benear

Chapter 23 – Happy Birthday Chris!

July 24, 2011 and July 25, 2011

Chris' trach was removed, on his birthday, July 25, 2011! We were so thankful and felt very fortunate that Chris had shown so much positive progress, but that day was difficult. Watching Chris being so upset and frustrated made that day very hard for his dad and me. A hospital is the last place anyone wants to be on their birthday. Chris turned twenty-eight that day and there he was in the hospital. As his parents, we saw how badly he felt about how his life was at that point, and it broke our hearts.

Stephanie's wedding was coming up that weekend and with Chris' birthday happening everyone's emotions were all over the place. The pressure Chris must have been feeling at that time about everything going on (birthday, wedding, rehab, work, home, etc.) must have been overwhelming for him. Chris had made so much progress, but he had such a long way to go and there was the constant question in all of our minds of 'how far could he go'? We could not put ourselves in Chris' shoes, but we knew how hard Chris had been on himself over the years to do everything at a high level, I was sure the uncertainty of his life must have been extremely hard and scary for him.

We tried to make Chris' hospital room a safe place by trying to keep all discussion pertaining to his condition and things happening outside of his control out of his presence. He seemed to be sleeping a lot, which he needed, but I also believed that it was his way of taking a break from everything happening to him and around him. We had wanted his room to be his escape so conversations on the Tigers, hunting, Gordon, friends, and anything that put a smile on his face were encouraged.

I was sure he understood everything that he was hearing and so wished he could have joined in the conversations, but we were all praying it would happen soon. One of the things Chris received from his mom is the gift that he could talk to anyone and we believed he would again.

The doctors had finally agreed four days after Chris' birthday that he could have some vanilla ice cream since his trach opening had healed so nicely. Chris had not had vanilla ice cream since June fourth (fifty-six days) which was usually a three to five times a week evening ritual. What a treat.

JOURNAL ENTRY – July 24th

Hi Chris

It is great spending time with you for your birthday (day before your birthday). I hope you like your camo blanket. I also was able to make you laugh a few times today too. ☺ You are amazing – the strongest person I know. You have taught me so much. I love ya buddy. John is still waiting to kick your a.. in ping pong. I can't wait to hear you talk again and for us to have our life chats. Keep fighting!

Love you – Sarah V

JOURNAL ENTRY – July 25th

Hi Chris

Happy birthday big guy. Good to see you today. I am amazed at the progress you've made in such a short time. Keep it up and you'll be out of here in no time. Then we can have a huge birthday party for you. I know it sucks being in the hospital let alone on your birthday. I feel for you bud. Wish I could do something to change the situation, but as you know, nobody can. Love you and miss you.

xoxox – Aunt Paula

JOURNAL ENTRY – July 25th

Happy Birthday Christopher

I know that this is not the way you would prefer to spend your birthday, but we're really thankful that you're here. Instead of dwelling on all of the bad, I'm going to think of all of the positive today. You've been through a lot and have come out better than we could ever have had a right to expect. We've had a miracle or two in the last couple of months. I'm thankful that you're alive and that you have come so far. And you continue to improve. Next year we'll be celebrating your birthday at home and this will all be just a memory...and I'll be thankful for that. So be thankful for everything that you have today! Love you!

Stacy

Chapter 24 – The Wedding

July 30, 2011

In the midst of all that was going on with Chris, Stephanie and Alex had pre-accident planned to get married on July 30, 2011 in Traverse City, Michigan. There was plenty of talk during the early days after Chris' accident of postponing the wedding to a later date. We had thought that if we postponed the date of the wedding, Chris could have been in the wedding as a groomsman as was originally planned. It would not have been the first wedding in our family to be postponed because of an accident.

Jeff and I were supposed to be married on September 23, 1978. On September fourth, Jeff had been riding his motorcycle from my parents' house to his parents' house. He had taken a road that was under construction for a new subdivision. There was dirt on the road from truck traffic. A rock was hidden from his view under the dirt.

His front tire had made it over the rock, but the back tire had hit the rock oddly and it had thrown Jeff off the bike.

His accident had resulted in a broken nose, two broken ankles, one broken leg, a broken shoulder blade, and four crushed vertebrae in his back. Needless to say, there was no wedding held for us on September twenty-third, it was postponed until December first.

Steph and Chris were so close that she had wanted nothing to do with going through with her wedding without her buddy being there with her. We went back and forth with the pros and cons of cancelling the wedding. One of the biggest factors in not cancelling the wedding was that Alex's family lived out of state and travel plans and hotels had already been booked.

The other major factor to consider was that we didn't know how long it would be before Chris recovered enough that he would be able to attend the wedding and participate. We could have moved the wedding date back, but until when? Alex was so supportive of Steph, he had said it was completely up to her to make the decision.

Jeff, at about two and a half weeks after the accident, had told Stephanie that she needed to proceed with all of her wedding plans. Her life could not be put on hold just because Chris had come to a bump in the road in his life. It was not fair to Alex, Stephanie, and both families to have to change all of their plans. We had no idea what the near future held for any of us, so it needed to happen as it had been scheduled. With tears rolling down her cheeks, she had hugged her dad; Stephanie had finally agreed to continue with the wedding as originally planned.

As Stephanie worked on preparations for the wedding, she had spent some nights with Chris in his hospital room. Trying to catch up on all of the loose ends that go with preparing for your wedding, she would type on her laptop late at night by his side as she thought he was sleeping. One night she told me Chris had become very agitated with her, and she couldn't understand why. He kept making noises and giving her dirty looks so she had questioned him about what she could possibly be doing that was so upsetting to him. Finally, he had lifted his hand and with his fingers acted like he was typing. "Is my working on my computer bothering you?" Steph had asked. Chris nodded yes, then went back to sleep.

I mentioned previously that Chris had always had very good hearing, and that since the accident, it had become so much more acute. Chris always hated when it was my turn to spend the night because of my snoring. I could count on being greeted in the middle of the night with a pillow or any other means he could use to get my attention. It appeared that typing and snoring were not his idea of nighttime music.

Stephanie and Alex were mowing some of Chris' lawns, and spending a lot of time at the hospital so there were small windows of time that she had been able to use for wedding details. Losing her wedding preparation time on the nights she spent with Chris had put more stress on her to get things done in time.

It was hard on her in a few areas because she had a vision in her head of what her wedding day would look like. Friends and cousins had offered to help with things that she had wanted to do herself. She chose to accept their kindness because she thought it was important to spend more time with Chris. The dress had been fitted, the venue had been set and paid for, and the minister had been secured. The only big unknown left had been who would stay with Chris at the hospital.

When John and Ronda B heard the wedding was a go, they had stepped right up and offered to stay at the hospital to be Chris' voice for the weekend. We were so thankful for that offer. Chris had always meant a lot to both of them, and the feeling was mutual. He would be in perfect hands. I had also found out my brother Robert said he would spend the weekend with my mom, so things were coming together. Family.

We left the hospital Friday around one, to make the three and a half hour drive to Traverse City. Rehearsal had been scheduled for around five, with dinner afterwards. Cousins and friends had shown up to the venue Saturday morning for decorating and set-up. With so many hands-on-deck, things seemed to go very smoothly.

Stephanie had planned for a signature drink for the toast, but forgot the ingredients. Without a missed beat, Judy D graciously went and picked up everything that was needed, including ice. I had made mini loaves of zucchini bread for favors, and the girls had added ribbon and a note from the bride and groom. The favors looked great. Stephanie and Alex had picked out wedding songs on the drive up to the venue, and a few additional last minute details were discussed. If you had asked me, I would have said that I thought things ran extremely smoothly, but I admit that I don't really know if I had been totally there at the time.

Sarah V offered to stay back and try to stream it live, so Chris could watch. He was able to see and talk to Stephanie before she walked down the aisle then the connection kept going out. Sarah finally gave up, but she was very persistent in helping Chris be a part of his sister's big day, until technology took over with a mind of its own. Looking back, it was probably for the best since Chris had been emotional when Jeff and I left the hospital, but he had tried hard to cover it up. Intense emotion could have been detrimental to his health if it affected him physiologically; we just hadn't known how his brain function would handle that emotion.

Jeff and I were both feeling bad for Chris because we knew he was emotionally hurting. It had been a very quiet ride up north. We had known it was an extremely difficult time for him missing his sister's wedding, but on the other hand we knew that he would have such great support while we were gone for those couple of days that this eased our minds.

I kept thinking, at the time, that it was the best decision for everyone to go forward with the wedding. Then I would wonder if we had done right by Chris. Every time I speak or think about my daughter getting married while my son was in the hospital the tears flow.

The wedding was beautiful. The groomsmen entered from the side, and left a space between them where Chris would have stood. Stephanie was absolutely stunning as her dad walked her down the aisle, and her bridesmaids were gorgeous. Alex looked very handsome as he waited for Stephanie. One of her favorite people had officiated the wedding which made what he said personal and especially meaningful. Dan D, the minister, had been her AAU basketball coach for years, and his daughter Lucy was one of her best friends. Lucy and Stephanie had played AAU and college basketball together, and were in each other's weddings. Over the years our families had become very close, and had spent a lot of good times together. When Dan agreed to go through classes so that he could officiate at her wedding, Stephanie was excited and relieved because the person marrying them knew them so well. She felt blessed.

It was hard taking pictures after the ceremony because our whole family wasn't there. Someone had asked Stephanie where her something blue was, she lifted the bottom of her dress, and there was a blue patch. The patch pinned to her dress had Chris' initials from one of the 'Built CB Tough' t-shirts they had had made for his fundraiser. She had happily shown anyone her patch, and the camouflage bracelet that said 'Fighting with Chris' that she never took off.

The reception was an awesome time filled with happiness, love, and lots of dancing. Jeff gave an emotional welcome speech where he talked about how thankful he was for all the love and support that our family had received from so many people who were gathered there that day. He had us crying and laughing as he talked about the relationship and adventures we had all gone through together. He had also thanked those of our family members that weren't there because they had helped out with watching over Chris so that we could celebrate Stephanie and Alex. Then Amanda, as the matron-of-honor, had continued with an amazing speech. She spoke of the bond between her, Stephanie, and Chris that had always been strong. She spoke of leaving for college, and how Stephanie and Chris had become closer and that their bond had become even stronger. She had mentioned that she was so proud of how Stephanie was helping take care of Chris, and of her strong parents who were holding them all together through a very hard time in their lives. She welcomed Alex into our family, and thanked him for stepping up to the plate, and helping out the last couple of months when extra help was needed. Amanda also told her sister that she loved and admired her for the person she had become.

Amanda and Jeff had both given speeches from the heart and they were delivered with pure raw emotion. I was so proud of them both for holding it together in those moments, and really coming through for Stephanie and Alex.

After the speeches we had some great food, and Alex and Stephanie danced their first dance as husband and wife. I felt like I completely lost it when Stephanie had picked Chris' favorite song,

'The Dance' sung by Garth Brooks, to be played for her 'Dad and Daughter Dance' in honor of him.

The tears seemed to flow easily the rest of the night, and from that 'Dad and Daughter Dance' on I just remember lots of <u>HUGs</u>.

'FIGHTING WITH CHRIS/BUILT TC TOUGH' POSTING – July 30th

A Thumbs up on the Dress

This weekend was a very emotional weekend and we all wished Chris could have been in Traverse City to celebrate his sister's wedding day with us. Instead, Chris stayed back in Ann Arbor with numerous friends and family members keeping him company throughout the days and nights, filling in for Chris' parents and siblings.

After debating whether or not he would want to *'Skype'*, Chris gave the thumbs up on the idea at the last minute on Saturday. Just minutes before Stephanie walked down the aisle, Stephanie was able to *'Skype'* with her brother to tell him how much she loved and missed him, how much she wished he was there, and to ask for his approval on the dress. His sister's wedding was a bit out in the boonies so the service was spotty, but his approval was clear. When asked about the dress, Chris gave her the thumbs up…putting the biggest smile ever on the bride-to-be's beautiful face. Just then Chris' dad came around the corner to walk his daughter down the aisle, and was able to say a few words to Chris as well. While he was a couple hundred miles away, the little time we had with him on *'Skype'* made us feel a bit more close to him.

Shortly after the ceremony began we lost connection with him, but he was with us in heart and spirit the whole day and night.

Thanks to all the friends and family members who helped make everything possible with Chris this week.

Emily B

Chapter 25 – Healing Times

August 5, 2011 through August 20, 2011

So many positive things happened this month with Chris's recovery it was hard to decide which to mention. More food choices, less medication (even though it hurt), and much needed trauma healing were part of his recovery process during these long days and nights.

'FIGHTING WITH CHRIS/BUILT TC TOUGH'
POSTING – August 5th

Good evening Christopher!

I haven't seen you for a week and I've been thinking about you every day. I'm used to seeing for myself how you are doing, but I've had to rely on second-hand information. I hear that you are still doing good. Tonight you are full of smiles. I've really missed your smile. You're showing your personality and humor by teasing Uncle John. It makes me so happy to see you being the

Chris we all know and love! I can't believe how far you've come in such a short amount of time. Keep up the great work.

See you again soon – ♡ Love Stacy

'FIGHTING WITH CHRIS/BUILT TC TOUGH'
POSTING – August 8th

Chris' menu is beginning to expand. With his trach hole almost completely healed, the doctors are starting to let Chris have the softer foods that are easy to process. He's enjoying anything from mac and cheese and cottage cheese to mashed potatoes and gravy. Of course a 'Frosty' from Wendy's still seems to be his favorite (vanilla only).

The doctors are also in the process of removing him from different antibiotics. And while the docs determine that he doesn't need some of the drugs, Chris is starting to determine some of the pain killers he doesn't want to take. It seems that he's found some of the drugs affect him enough that they hold him back in therapy. Realizing that he's not able to perform as well as he would like, he seems to be choosing pain over not performing. Gosh, what a guy... We're continuously in awe of him!

Team Benear

'FIGHTING WITH CHRIS/BUILT TC TOUGH'
POSTING – August 11ᵗʰ

Today there's even more exciting news…the doctors removed his last IV! This is a HUGE step! Without any IV's in his way, Chris will be much more comfortable and will be bothered even less throughout the days and nights. This also means that the only thing still hooked up to Chris is his feeding tube. With Chris eating more and more these days, the doctors are beginning to think that it won't be much longer before the feeding tube can be removed too!

Wow! We have so much to be thankful for! Your prayers are working!

Team Benear

'FIGHTING WITH CHRIS/BUILT TC TOUGH'
POSTING – August 20ᵗʰ

You've got to love sibling love!

Today, Amanda, Chris' sister walked into Chris' room and went straight for a hug from Chris. Little did she know she was going to have to work for that hug. When she leaned in for the hug, Chris just gave her a little smirk and looked the other way (something he does quite often to his sisters). Thinking that she could get him, Amanda challenged Chris to an arm wrestling match saying that if she wins she gets a hug from him whenever she wants one. Chris, who never turned a dare down, accepted the challenge.

After a few stretches to prepare herself, Amanda and Chris put their left elbows on a table and counted down to one. Poor Amanda, the stretches didn't do much. In no time at all, Chris had Amanda pinned. Although he knew that he would be giving Amanda a hug eventually, Chris just couldn't help but remind her that he's still in control.

He may be Amanda's younger brother, but he's still bigger and stronger!

Team Benear

Chapter 26 – Hospital Rehab Day after Day

July 6, 2011 through September 13, 2011

For 70 days Chris had gone through intense therapies day after day. Sundays had usually been an off day, but if there was anything available Chris would sign up.

Occupational therapists had worked with Chris on every day skills he would need so that he could go home and eventually be on his own. Chris' right hand had not shown signs of useful functioning so most of that time had been spent on strengthening his left hand. They tried to incorporate things that Chris loved to do; playing card games, board games, and hunting video games, grilling, and other life skills which would help to improve his hand coordination and build back up the strength that he had lost.

Speech therapists had started out by using different signs, spelling words on an alphabet folder (which Vanessa had made him), and flash cards. Then Chris graduated to an iPad for spelling and communicating. He had struggled with his voice, but after the trach came out, a lot of work had been done with his vocabulary. It was great to hear small sounds coming out, and that had given us a lot of optimism about Chris' speech coming back. We had been told at the beginning that Chris might never talk again. We were witnessing another miracle at work.

Physical therapists had covered all of Chris' physical movement recovery. Every day Chris would complete all three therapies then head back up to his room for lunch and a nap before he would repeat all three therapies over again in the afternoon. The doctors had explained that this would be one of the hardest stages in Chris' recovery process, and wow were they right.

Chris had mentally seemed to be ready and willing to handle a lot, but physically he had not been ready. Fatigue set in fast. How long would Chris' recovery process take?

Chris had spelled out his questions for the docs, "How long before I can walk and talk doc?" They didn't seem to have any answers that satisfied Chris. They just explained to him that the brain is complicated, and that everyone heals differently. They had known he was very frustrated, but they assured him that they were right there with him, and would help him get through the struggles. They tried to help him with his frustration levels by using tips and setting new goals that he was able to look forward to reaching. The doctor kept repeating, "One step at a time Chris, your recovery is going to be a marathon, not a sprint!"

I remember being in Chris' PT session when they had stood Chris up for the first time. WOW. It took five people to stand him up and steady him which had been for just a few seconds. It was so heartbreaking seeing Chris doing something he, and all of us, had taken for granted and what a struggle it had been just for him to stand for a few seconds. Although not even standing on his own, it was exhilarating to see Chris stand at all, something we had been warned early on might not happen. What a great milestone!

Once they had built up Chris' stamina and balance, his walking adventures were a sight to see. Chris would walk with a rolling walker and a troop of three; two therapists and an assistant with a full length mirror. Chris along with the two physical therapists, one in front of him and one in back to support him, had all worked together to go about thirty to forty feet down the hall. Around fifteen feet ahead of the trio there had been an assistant who kept moving a full length mirror so that Chris could see what he was doing (without looking down). We had constantly been able to hear the therapists encouraging him:

"Keep your head up Chris!"

"Keep your eyes on the mirror Chris!"

"Take a bigger step with your left Chris!"

"Stand up straight Chris!"

"Help us move that right foot Chris!"

"Chris, Chris, Chris…"

What patience and determination Chris demonstrated with everything that was being thrown at him. The PTs and Chris were all business, but every once in a while Chris would give them a smirk and everyone would crack up and laugh, then back to business. When they finally made it to the end of the hall, the group had turned around and they would do it all over again. On a good day, they would make about three trips down the hall before calling it quits. Chris was very responsive as he listened to every therapist as they were working with him. All of the encouragement from the staff had helped him as he fought through the pain and frustration he felt. His strength, courage and determination were unbelievable!

Day after day Chris faced and overcame new hurdles. Things that he used to take for granted that he could do were coming back so slowly. Chris had a hard time seeing progress, but we could see him progressing and were thankful for every step he took.

He seemed to get along with almost every therapist, but Larry and Chris seemed to have a good bond that formed quickly. Larry was the main physical therapist assigned to Chris so they spent a lot of time together. I had noticed them giving each other winks, thumbs up, smirks, and high fives at the weirdest times. Come to find out, when an attractive woman walked by, all the shenanigans started. Coach was another special person Chris had met. He seemed to have a fatherly way of handling Chris, and had seemed to have a great rapport with him.

When it was time to leave the hospital, there were doctors, nurses, and therapists we would surely miss, but we were so ready to be moving on with Chris' recovery <u>marathon</u>!

'FIGHTING WITH CHRIS/BUILT TC TOUGH' POSTING – August 26th

A Fantastic Day in Physical Therapy

Today Chris had a fantastic day in physical therapy. Without anyone touching him, he took five steps on his own! As everyone is fully aware, this is a huge accomplishment.

Chris is an inspiration to us all!

Team Benear

Chapter 27 – Home Sweet Home

September 13, 2011 to September 14, 2011

After 100 days at the University of Michigan hospital following Chris' car accident, we were finally getting ready to bring him home. They had given us some different options for Chris' continued recovery efforts, but the only thing I knew for sure was that we wanted to bring him home. Chris would be back in an environment that would be familiar, and we would do everything we could to make it comfortable and safe.

Social Services had sent someone on a home visit to check on what would be best for Chris' living arrangements. Chris' house was three stories with a wooden staircase to reach the upper and lower levels. Our home was a ranch with only one step up into the main level from a lower family room. The decision made was that our home would work so much easier for the early stages of his rehab. After extra railings were installed, and bathroom bars had been added for safety, we felt ready. The only drawback would be that Chris would have to sleep next door to our bedroom. I snore.

I was excited that Amanda and her family could come on the weekends to spend quality time with Chris. Stephanie could easily come after work, and she always had a special way with Chris through his ups and downs. Family and friends could stop by for a visit more easily than making the trip to the hospital. After the emotional roller coaster our whole extended family had been on for the last three months, I could not stop smiling on the drive to bring my 'little boy' home. We can do this as a family.

Wednesday

September 14, 2011

Jeff had spent the night before with Chris and he called me to say that his release would definitely be that day and that it would happen soon. I was so excited after everything that Chris had been through that he had been cleared to be released to come home.

Chris had only left the hospital prior to his release for a day trip to a nearby park with the rehabilitation program in early August, but on his release, just the long ride to get home took a lot out of him. When we arrived home, we took things very slowly. Chris found a favorite spot on the end of the couch that reclined. When he tried to sleep, we kept it as quiet as we could, and tried to make him as comfortable as possible.

He had to use a walker to get around in the house which was hard on him. Even though he had been in rehab for ten weeks, he had still been very weak. His first trip to the bathroom was very hard to watch. Chris had been trying to go through the door and his walker wouldn't fit. I heard the banging on the door and walls as he tried to get through the door frame. Jeff had hurried to go help Chris and he realized the wheels on the walker were on the outside which he explained to Chris. He told him that he would move the wheels to the inside which would allow the walker to fit more easily. Chris' frustration had boiled over on his way back to the living room. In the middle of the room he had broken down crying and just stood there. What could I have said or done to help him besides saying, "Chris, it will get better." Amanda, who had been spending the day with us walked up and just hugged him. No more words were spoken for a while. The neurosurgeons, therapists, doctors, and nurses had all told me at different times that there would be a lot of ups and downs during recovery from a brain injury.

Chris' frustration level on completing daily tasks that he used to take for granted was so hard for this mom to witness. The first couple of days had been full of highs and lows, friends and family visits, and home-made goodies delivered with lots of smiles and hugs. We also had tears coming from both bedrooms in the middle of the night, clearly heard when things were so quiet. I remember Jeff going into Chris' room in the early morning hours and reassuring him that everything was going to be okay, it was just going to take time. Then he had come back into our room where we hugged each other tightly.

'FIGHTING WITH CHRIS/BUILT TC TOUGH'
POSTING – September 14ᵗʰ

Three months ago our worlds changed forever…Chris' more than anyone else's.

With Chris' hard work and your prayers though, Chris is going home! By no means does this mean the struggle is over. It simply means that he will be sleeping in a more comfortable bed, and doing his daily therapies outside of the U of M walls. From home, Chris will continue to kick butt, and we will continue to need your prayers. Please know that we know that we could not have gone through this tough experience without you and we thank you from the bottom of our hearts for all of your continued support. You all are truly a blessing!

Team Benear

It had been a very long few months filled with the ups and downs of Chris' accident, surgery, taking care of business, and constant hoping and praying for his full recovery. The worries had been exhausting, not only about Chris, but my mother too.

Chapter 28 – Jean – Mom – Grandma

Days, Weeks, and Months through October of 2011

It had been since June fourteenth, Chris' surgery day, that I had received a hug from my mom, Jean, so Jeff and I stopped by to visit her on a Saturday night a few weeks later when Chris had a full posse spending the night with him. It was the first time mom had seen Jeff since the accident. They had become very close over the years. Mom was Jeff's sponsor when he became a Catholic, and she was the one that offered to have him come recuperate at her house after his motorcycle accident, before our wedding. When we walked in, mom gave Jeff an especially long and solid hug before I received mine.

We found seats at the big round oak table in the kitchen where a lot of meals had been shared; cards; Spoons; and other games had been won and lost; deer processing happened; and coffee, tea, gossip, and stern lectures had been doled out as mom had visited with friends and family. A lot of love had been shared over the years around that oak table. If only it could talk, what a history it could share.

As we sat around the table visiting, a few more people had stopped in, and soon the table was covered with drinks and a lot of chairs were filled. Mom seemed to be happiest when the table was full. We had talked a little about everything, and then had tried to explain all that Chris had been going through, keeping it as positive as possible. She had been getting updates every day from my sisters and nieces, but hearing it straight from Jeff and me seemed to make her feel better. Our mom was a very smart person, and I knew she was reading between the lines for what we weren't saying.

What was supposed to have been a short visit had turned into hours, but as we were leaving, I remember feeling a peace of mind that things were going to be okay. I had promised mom that I would stop by more often, and she had promised to keep praying. When my siblings and I were growing up, my parents had said the rosary every night before they went to sleep. There had been some nights that six or seven little ones would be all around their bed kneeling on the floor joining in. Most nights we had already been sent to bed before they headed to their room, but we could hear them from upstairs saying the familiar prayers. Once in a while I would come home late, and would join them half way through the rosary. They would always make me feel so special for joining them. When mom promised to keep praying, I knew I could count on her saying her prayers. When Jeff and I walked out to the car that evening I looked up at the stars and I knew that dad had been with us the whole night.

In the next few months, every time I had really needed a good hug, I would stop by my mom's even if it was only for a short visit. I so appreciated my sisters for covering all the extra hours of care with my mom so that I could be where I needed to be, with my son. Mom had been so understanding of my short visits, she always made me feel better and more hopeful before I left. Even though I had known she wasn't feeling well, she never complained about her health to me during my visits, she had only shown her concern for Chris' recovery. Mom had not been traveling at all since we had brought hospice into her home. Before I left, she always gave me a big hug, and would say, "Share that with Jeff, Amanda, Stephanie, and Chris when you see them." Mom was no longer been able to travel to give them hugs herself.

I promised my mom that I would bring Chris over for a visit when he was released from the hospital and he was up for it. Around three weeks after Chris had come home in September, we were on our way home from therapy when I asked Chris if he wanted to go see Grandma. He had nodded yes, so we drove on by our house, and headed straight to grandma's house.

I grew up on a big farm, and when Jeff and I were looking for a house, my parents had offered us an acre of land on the back end of the farm. My dad thought that if we were on the other side of the river and the cows got through the fence we could put them back inside the fence. For years, my garden had always been the first one they hit when they found a hole in their fence line. We were so fortunate and blessed to be able to raise our three children where it had literally been through the woods and over the river to grandma's house they could go.

Chris and I passed our house and drove the mile to my mom's house in just a couple of minutes. We walked in the back door and were greeted by one of my sisters. I could see mom sitting in her chair in the front room. Chris had headed into the front room and you could see mom's eyes light up as she said, "Chris." He walked over to grandma, bent over, and gave her a huge, but gentle, hug. We set a chair down by my mom for Chris, and they just sat next to each other as my mom had grabbed his hand. Mom was crying, Chris was crying, and I couldn't hold it together. Nothing had been said for what seemed like forever. Finally, she told Chris she loved him, and said that she was so happy he had come to visit.

After some time passed, mom and Chris hugged goodbye and Chris headed out back toward the car. As mom and I hugged, she told me she thought Chris looked good, and thanked me for bringing him over. I promised we would be back.

I drove Chris home, and the rest of our evening was very quiet. We had both been drained from such an emotional visit. Chris loved his grandma so much. They had teamed up as partners in a lot of card games. Chris had mowed her lawn, cut wood for her, and helped her out in any way he could before his accident. Grandma had also always been very excited when Chris had a successful hunt and had come to the house to share it with her. They had just enjoyed each other's company.

A few weeks after that visit, mom took a turn for the worse and quit eating. I had known it would be hard on Chris, but he wanted to go see her again so we went over on October thirtieth. Chris sat by the edge of her bed for what seemed like hours just staring at her, every once in a while he rubbed her arm. She had been unresponsive, just sleeping, but in my heart I felt that she had known Chris was there.

Two days later, three of my siblings had been with me by her bedside as she quietly passed away on November 1, 2011. When we had lost our dad it was hard, but to lose a second parent seemed so much worse. My family is not perfect, but we pulled it all together to give our mom a beautiful send-off to be with our dad. Chris was not comfortable being around a lot of people yet. It had been hard on him to go to the funeral home and the church. He was not talking much, was still wearing the helmet, and maneuvering around people was a challenge for him, but he had done it to honor her. His grandma was a lady he looked up to, respected, and loved.

Our girls also loved their grandma. The girls and Chris were always excited when she had attended their sporting events, plays, musicals, birthday parties, and had loved being at grandma's house. My mom's passing was hard on all of us and with everything we had been through together in the last five months, we were all struggling.

Our mom was a great mom, and a wonderful grandma to so many. She had also been loved by her co-workers and neighbors and had loved them right back. Now I believe my mom and dad are the shining stars I see while I sit on the swing and gaze at the night sky. She has been our angel watching over all of us for the last ten years as we learn to live with our new normal. I know she is up there smiling from ear to ear every time Chris beats me at a game of cards, which she taught him to play. She had always been so happy whenever any of the hunters in the family (especially the grandkids) bagged a buck and couldn't wait for them to drive up to the window so she could get a look. Now she smiles down on them and their trophies.

I only hope and pray that Jeff and I, as parents, have shown our children that they have been given the same unconditional love we were given growing up, and that hard work and being a person of your word pays off in the long run as you go through your life journey. Most importantly, that an honest and sincere hug means the world to both the giver and the receiver of that hug.

Chapter 29 – Willowbrook Outpatient Therapy

September 14, 2011 through July 24, 2015

Chris was released from the hospital on September 14, 2011. Before we left the hospital, they wanted us to have a neurologist, a physical medicine and rehabilitation doctor, and a rehabilitation facility all in place. We had taken a lot of recommendations and had begun to check out doctors and facilities. Everything was so new and unknown because we were going through this situation for the first time. Listening to other peoples' referrals was so important.

After phone calls and some investigation, the first place we had checked out in person was Willowbrook in Brighton, Michigan. The commute would be an easy 20 minute drive each way and we could keep Chris at home with us since we could do outpatient. They came highly recommended. About two weeks before Chris was expected to be released from the hospital we went and visited with the staff and toured the Willowbrook facility. The therapist seemed very friendly which meant a lot. We met Margie, who would be in charge of Chris' schedule, her demeanor was so positive I really thought Chris would like her. I had explained to her about Chris' accident, his determination to have a complete recovery, and a little about his personality. I also mentioned Chris' lack of patience for anything other than fast results, but that she would not find a harder worker. He is a great kid. (He was a young man, but always my kid.) I had been happily comfortable with letting them know that we would be bringing him there, but that Chris would have to feel comfortable for us to stay.

After Chris had been released from the hospital, which was on a Wednesday, Margie had said that they would be expecting him on Monday morning, September 19th at 9:00 a.m.

Monday

September 19, 2011

On Monday, we had arrived at Willowbrook around 8:40 a.m. Chris always liked to be early. I had pushed Chris into the center in a wheelchair not knowing how far he would have to walk. His first few days at home had been very exhausting for him. He was tired before he even started therapy that day. I had been told I could come back at noon for his lunch break and then needed to be back around 3:00 p.m. to pick him up. As I walked out of the facility, I felt so nervous about leaving him there in case he needed something or needed me. I had given them my number. I could have been back within minutes if I had stayed in town, but I chose to sit in the parking lot. I only left to get Chris lunch, and was back sitting inside the facility by 11:50 waiting for Chris to come down to eat.

I was so happy to find out that Chris and Margie had hit it off right from the beginning. Margie explained to me that she had met Chris before. While Chris and Margie were sitting in the gym at Willowbrook, Chris had spelled out A C T I O N on his letter board. In trying to figure out what Chris had meant by that word, she asked Chris if he wanted to move. He then started to point outside. It took her a few minutes, after asking some questions, to realize that he was pointing outside because he had been out there before while working for ACTION. ACTION was the electrical company where Chris had worked with her ex-husband. They had stopped by Willowbrook to leave Margie some papers a few years ago. Chris and Margie had briefly met that day. Obviously he had looked a little different and was not wearing a helmet then, but she remembered that day. Chris had also recognized that one of the therapists was a girl who had graduated from high school with him. He had acknowledged her with a nod and a small smile. Small world.

In trying to write about what happened in the next four years of rehabilitation at Willowbrook, I decided it was best to get some help. I had asked Margie if she could give me Chris' records which included evaluations, testing, doctor appointments, medicine changes, and everything you could possibly think of regarding his condition just after the accident, his release from the hospital, and during rehab.

Chris signed a paper to okay the report being given to me. I was so excited to get some extra help from the information in the report. Wow, wow, wow, it was a new language to learn. The first things I read in the initial evaluation brought back some pretty awful memories:

Chris was hospitalized at the University of Michigan Medical Center (UMMC) with the following findings:

- Verbal responsiveness in the field; use of R side: GCS=7,
- CT of the head revealed penetrating trauma with depressed fracture and large foreign body (piece of tree wood) traversing the left parietal lobe with associated parenchymal, subarachnoid, and subdural hemorrhages,
- leg wounds secondary to crawling over natural and road debris,
- tracheostomy and G tubes placed on 6/9/11 (resolved),
- surgery on 6/14/11 included L decompressive hemicraniectomy; removal of foreign bodies; and repair of scalp laceration,
- ICU course complicated by fevers; infected leg ulcers; and aspiration pneumonia,
- ventilator discontinued on 6/24/11,

- transfer to Acute Rehab on 6/30/11. RLAS was 2-3 with no visual tracking,
- G tube removed on 8/29/11, placed on regular diet with thin liquids (VFSS completed on 7/27/11),
- progressed to RLAS 6-7 by 9/8/11,
- discharge from the rehab unit on 9/13/11 to his parents' home (9/14/11). Family is providing 24/7 attendant care,
- mother was awarded guardianship and conservatorship,
- admission to WBRS (outpatient) on 9/19/11.

Then I read through his past medical history and rehab staff observations:

- R, ACL reconstruction with mild osteoarthritis of the R knee joint,
- intramedullary nailing in the L tibia,
- screw placement in the L fifth metatarsal base,
- mild past traumatic deformity of the proximal shaft of the L fibula and mid to distal shaft of the L tibia.

Observations Summary:

Christopher Benear is a twenty-eight year old (07/25/1983) single male who sustained a severe traumatic brain injury secondary to a single vehicle accident. He attended sessions with ambulation assistance. Chris eventually progressed to independent ambulation with a cane and SBA. Chris has an obvious R hemiparesis with currently nonfunctional RUE (he was right hand dominant before injury).

There is a L side cranium indentation (covered when out of bed by a protective helmet). Cranial flap replacement is pending. Chris is primarily nonverbal although over sessions he did attempt single word articulation with success. His tone was flat and volume forceful. The primary communication device used was a letter board until the very recent addition of an iPad which Chris is just learning how to use.

Chris' emotional presentation during evaluation sessions ranged from neutral/blunted to mildly animated, which is reasonable considering his circumstances and the limited number of sessions attended to date. He has no frame of reference for the therapeutic experience, and is understandably wary of purpose and benefit. We have lightly discussed the recovery process (physical, cognitive, and emotional), and how his injury has impacted family and friends as well. Chris is offered choices of topic each session, and it is hoped that his enhanced communication options will segue into his initiating questions and information.

PT

Physical movements most of us take for granted each day were a struggle for Chris and had to be relearned with part of his body not cooperating. For physical therapy they monitor and work on posture, muscle tone, sensation, reflexes, flexibility, range of motion, strength, gait, endurance, balance, and coordination among other areas.

Long term goals were to improve his mobility and balance so that Chris could walk on level/uneven surfaces and stairs independently and safely using a device if needed. They also wanted his overall endurance and right lower extremity strength, flexibility, and range of motion to improve to 'Good' for daily activities function.

OT

Occupational Therapy involved monitoring and working on muscle tone, range of motion, hand dominance, fine motor skills, sensory motor processing skills, visual perception and acuity, safety and judgment, and community integration. He needed to make improvements or relearn in most areas.

Long term goals were to increase strength and fine motor skills, improve visual perception, demonstrate knowledge of medications with 80% accuracy, and resume independence safely in select community, literacy, household tasks, and with meal preparations.

SP

Speech communication was a high priority. They assessed auditory comprehension, reading comprehension, graphic expression, verbal expression, oral motor/swallowing, attention and memory, orientation, and organization/sequencing. Chris' capabilities at that point ranged from mild, moderate, to severe impairment depending on the area. In his initial evaluation he presented with very little speech output.

Long term goals were for Chris to complete exercises which would improve intelligibility, produce functional phrases, complete reading comprehension tasks, improve written expression, maintain attention to tasks for up to 30 minutes, and complete basic organization and memory tasks.

Wow, wow, wow that was a lot to read, comprehend, and digest. Chris had been through so much and it was really hard reading the details of everything my 'little boy' had gone through early on. It has been ten years, and the tears flow easily just reading through what Chris has had to endure.

I had taken a year off work so that I could take Chris to his therapy appointments every day. I thanked God that we were in a position that I could take a year off. My work was really good about it, but I would have done whatever I needed to do for my family. We arrived early every day because Chris hated to be late. At first, I had gone to get lunch or had packed it and had been back to eat with Chris. At the beginning, Chris hadn't wanted anything to do with the other patients. He tried to keep to himself, and had just concentrated on his sessions. Then eventually he felt more relaxed and his personality started to show back up. He had become comfortable staying in the lunch room to eat lunch.

For the first year, I planned my days depending on what Chris had planned to do for lunch. He had really needed to eat well to keep up his strength for his sessions, especially his physical therapy. After lunch he would go to a side room off the gym area and catch a few zzz's. Even if it was for only ten to twenty minutes, that rest had really helped his concentration for the remainder of the day. When I had to return to work, his lunch consisted of going out to eat with Aunt Nancy or a therapist. There were days he would order in something with the help of a therapist, fix something in occupational therapy with assistance, or bag it which was the least of his favorites. If lunch was good, the day just flowed a lot easier for him.

Willowbrook Highlights –

- Chris made a lot of friends.
- The gym started to play a lot more country music.
- Chris was stubborn – there were things he didn't want to try because he didn't think it would help. His determination to get better eventually won out and he tried everything.
- The staff learned never to fake understanding Chris. If he thought you had no idea what he was saying, but you acted like you did, he would say, "What did I say?" After they would turn red, he would try again.
- Chris made remarkable progress.

- Speech drills were barely tolerated, but tolerated.
- Chris taught Beth that wild blackberries were safe to eat. He would feast on them every time they would walk outside and the berries were available.
- A friendly, dedicated staff.
- Chris had started there by communicating with head nods, thumbs up/down, letter board, or iPad; he left being able to put sentences together.
- In an early evaluation, Chris was timed on a six-minute walk – 32.5 feet accomplished. At discharge, on a six-minute walk he accomplished 2032 feet. (Average for most people is 2618 feet.)
- Berg balance Assessment – Chris started at 27/56 and ended at 53/56.
- Chris' weight start was 171.5, and ended at 192.0.
- Chris was pleasant and cooperative throughout his course of treatment and consistently put forth maximal effort with his PT program.

By no means do I want to devalue the progress Chris made at Willowbrook by not going into more detail. But, if I attempted to show you more detail in how much he improved in the four years he was a patient there, this book would never end.

Chris had been at Willowbrook from September 19, 2011 to July 24, 2015 going every day for the first three and a half years from 9:00 a.m. to 3:30 p.m. Then he had plateaued out in early 2015, going less and less until he was discharged. By the time Chris had plateaued out of Willowbrook, he had achieved or approximated some goals sooner than others for PT, OT, and Speech, but his relearning of life skills, speech, mobility, range of motion, gait, strength, flexibility, endurance, balance, grip, muscle tone, and coordination had all significantly improved.

Outpatient therapy was a daily struggle for Chris as every session that he had participated in over those four years had caused him additional stress, aches, and pains amidst the achievements. He had such determination, he just had to keep the positive in mind for at the end of all that struggle was a chance to regain some of the life skills he valued most. We had also made new and lasting friendships that we will always cherish. Although things seemed to be going really well considering all that had happened, we were in for another surprise.

Chapter 30 – Seizures

May 13, 2012

Shortly after Chris' accident he was put on seizure medication. It had really puzzled me as to why he needed medicine for seizures. Chris, to my knowledge, had never had a seizure. Did they think that was what had caused the accident?

The hospital staff had informed us that it wasn't IF he would have a seizure, it was WHEN he would have a seizure. The doctors had informed us that medical research showed that the majority of patients that have had to have brain surgery end up having seizures.

It was May 13th, not quite a year since Chris' accident and I had secretly hoped that seizures were one thing we might never have to deal with. My hopes were dashed as that day progressed.

Seizure #1

For Mother's day 2012 all of our kids and their families had been at our home celebrating Mother's day with me. It was bitter-sweet because although my whole family was there, it was the first Mother's day without my mom.

Jeff and the guys had barbequed and put on a pretty impressive spread of food. After the guys had cleaned up we headed outside to the swing where the kids were giving me some awesome hanging baskets when I heard Amanda yell, "Chris, that hurts." I turned around and watched as Chris had grabbed Amanda's shoulder. It appeared that he was having a seizure.

Amanda said that she thought Chris was teasing her when he had grabbed her shoulder, but as she turned around to tell him it hurt, she realized that something wasn't right. She grabbed Chris to steady him as Jeff, Justin, and Alex ran to assist her. As a unit, they all held Chris for a minute or so until he came back around. Someone brought a chair over and they sat Chris down.

In those minutes, Chris' six feet four inch body had become very stiff. His head had gone back a little to one side, and while he mumbled, his eyes had rolled up. That had frightened all of us! Although he had seemed to come out of it relatively quickly, I had called 911. We moved him inside to the couch. Wow was he mad when the ambulance arrived and he found out that I had called 911. That's what moms do.

The paramedics had a real hard time getting Chris to answer questions or let them take his vitals. He was so angry that he had a seizure, and he was mad at me for them being there. Finally the paramedic told Chris that either they could do some vitals there or they could transport him to the hospital. The hospital was not an option for him, in his mind, so Chris cooperated.

The medics had thought everything looked good at that point and recommended he follow up with his doctor in the morning. He was told they would probably want blood work.

In the morning we called his neurologist who sent us for a blood draw. They then adjusted his medications which were still considered a therapeutic dose.

July 31, 2012

Seizure #2

I usually drove Chris back and forth to rehab in Brighton which was around 16 miles each way. We were not quite half way there on this day when I had asked Chris a question and received no answer. I turned to my right to look at him and could tell Chris was having a seizure so I pulled over and I kept talking to him. Soon he had come out of it and we proceeded to rehab.

They did a blood draw and increased his medication slightly, but I made no 911 call…I was learning!

November 18, 2012

Seizure #3

John B and Jeff had taken Chris up to deer camp in Lewiston, Michigan. Deer camp was a tradition that had been repeated year after year since Chris had turned fourteen. Even if you couldn't hunt, the camp experience was worth the three hour drive.

It was early afternoon. Everyone was out of the woods and Chris was sitting on the couch when this seizure started. He had the same symptoms as the first seizure; blank stare and mumbling. Jeff and John had continued to talk to him, hold his arm, and told him he was all right and that they were there with him. They took him to Lewiston, had his blood drawn, and had the results forwarded to his neurologist. We had learned early on that a blood test as soon as possible would help them determine if his meds needed to be adjusted.

Chris' speech was not great at this point in his rehabilitation, but John had asked him if he knew where he was. Chris had responded CABIN as clear as before the accident. John and Jeff were both amazed.

January 15, 2013

Seizure #4

Chris had been at Willowbrook for rehab therapy that day, and it was lunch time. He had just gone into the restroom when the aide had heard Chris groan. This seizure had lasted around a minute and a half so when I arrived back to the center, I took him for another blood draw and made another call to the neurologist. It was time for another medicine change.

March 11, 2013

Seizure #5

John and Jeff were at Chris' house that day. This seizure lasted around two minutes. When he had come around, he knew where he was and said that he had felt it coming on. They increased his medication.

March 25, 2013

Seizure #6

Chris was at rehab when he told his therapist that he felt a little weird. Later that day, he had trouble speaking. It was determined that he had a very small seizure without all the symptoms being as vivid. Because of this seizure, they decided to add a sub therapeutic amount of a new seizure medicine.

June 20, 2014

Seizure #7

The Boat ('knock on wood')…

As bad as Chris' first seizure had been, his last one, as of the writing of this book, was the worst. Every time I tell this story we 'knock on wood' hoping that it will be the last one.

Jack, our grandson, had been staying over for his week at 'Camp Benear' (our house). He would come for a week during the summer to spend some fun times with Grandma, Grandpa, and Uncle Bean. 'Camp Benear' usually consisted of a basketball camp at the high school, eating out once or twice, lots of playing in the woods, and fishing.

It was his last day at 'camp' so Grandpa and Uncle Bean were taking him fishing. Jack had turned six that year and he couldn't wait to help get everything loaded. They were off! He knew that when he arrived back to our house his mom and dad would be waiting so this was his last adventure with just him and the big guys for a while.

They were going two miles down the road to a private five acre lake. Chris had mowed the owner's lawn for years so she let him keep a boat there, and he and his dad had fished in it off and on for years. They were loading the boat when Jeff realized that they had forgotten

Jack's life jacket. He called me to ask if I could bring it down to them. "Absolutely," I replied, "I'll be right there."

Jack had seen me coming toward the lake so he ran up the lawn toward me. He was so excited. I helped him put his life jacket on, he said, "Thanks Grandma," and he was gone, running back to the lake. I watched for a little while as Chris, using his left arm and hand, had been running the trolling motor and Grandpa and Jack were baiting the hooks.

It had rained in the early morning hours so they were getting a late start, but it was turning into a beautiful day with a full sun. The lake had sparkled.

I had gone home and Amanda and the rest of her family arrived. Their other children were four year old Kate, and Elle who was just seven months old. We had all planned to go to a family wedding the next day so they were spending the night. As we had started preparing a late lunch, everything seemed normal. Then the back door burst open with Jeff and Jack entering soaking wet on their way into the living room. "Where's Chris," I had asked because I knew he had planned on coming back for lunch. Jeff started to break down as he told us that there had been an accident. "Chris is fine. I took him home so he could change clothes, and rest for a while."

Jeff and Jack both broke down crying so I immediately hugged Jeff as Amanda grabbed Jack. Jeff told us that Chris had a seizure when they were fishing, and then explained what had happened…

They had not been having much luck in the middle of the lake so Jeff had asked Chris to get them closer to the shore. There was no response. Jeff waited another few seconds then he said, "Hey Chris." As he turned around, he noticed that Chris was having a seizure. Chris was stiff and mumbling, and had started to tip over. Jeff jumped up to grab Chris, who wasn't wearing a life jacket, and the boat flipped over! Jack went flying. Chris and Jeff went into the water, both going under. Jeff's instincts took over. He knew that he needed to get Chris up and out of the water or he might drown. Chris (6' 4" and 180 lbs.) had started flailing, and Jeff (5' 10") struggled just to get Chris to the surface of the water because Chris was dead weight at the time. Jeff had gotten a hold of Chris when he heard Jack yelling for him. Jeff responded saying, "Jack you're going to be fine, just swim over here to the boat buddie."

Chris started coming out of the seizure and realized what was going on as Jeff had almost gotten the two of them to the boat. With Jeff still holding on to him, Chris was able to get his left arm up on the boat to hang on as Jeff held on to Chris' other side and started paddling toward shore. Jack was a trooper as he was trying to kick and help pull the upside down boat to shore from the other side of the boat.

They had been about one hundred feet from the shore and Chris had stayed afloat by holding onto the boat. Amazing! Jeff had used all the strength he had to kick and paddle with one side as he was still holding onto Chris. When they had reached the shore totally exhausted, they had all flopped down. Chris had not had a seizure for over a year so no one was thinking about a life jacket for either of the big guys being a priority, they could both swim. I can't imagine how much harder it had been for them to make it back to shore without their life preservers on.

When they had recovered enough to speak, Grandpa said to Jack, "You okay?" "Yes, Grandpa," Jack had said. Grandpa replied, "You did great buddy!" As they climbed into the truck, Chris had said that he wanted to go home to dry off and be alone for a few minutes.

After tears were shed and blessings counted, I hugged Jeff again; amazed at the strength and courage it must have taken to handle that situation.

Justin decided that he would go sit with Chris at his house. We were so thankful for his thoughtfulness. We knew that Chris just needed some time to let everything set in, but we were all still worried about him. Not only was he trying to take in the fact that there could have been serious repercussions for him from his fall into the lake, but that there had been possible repercussions for others.

He could have drowned. His dad and nephew could have been hurt. Having survived his fall into the lake, it still felt like a door closed on the life he was building because when you have a seizure, you are not allowed to drive for six months. This trampled on the independence he felt he was finally getting back.

Again, as of this writing, this was Chris' last seizure ('knock on wood'). I thank you Jesus. Thank you for keeping an extra eye on my three men that day.

Chapter 31 – Chris' Personality

Chris' sense of humor before his accident was positive and playful. Easy to talk to and kid friendly, he had a great way with older people and youngsters, and was a little mischievous at times. I was so afraid that he would lose that special ingredient that made Chris so unique because of his brain injury. It never left!!

Chris' personality was pretty easy to pick up on as time went by which endeared him to many people he came in contact with during his recovery process. I know I am Chris' mom, and might be a little biased, but I really don't know too many people who don't like Chris.

When one of his therapists said he could probably beat him in basketball one on one when Chris is back up and moving well, Chris gave him a (yeah right) grin. He would pretend to be asleep when his sisters would ask for hugs. Then someone else would walk in and he would be wide awake. He was such a tease. One day the patients participating in the rehabilitation program at U of M had taken a day trip to a park accompanied by some nurses and assistants. They feasted on a picnic and then enjoyed a paddle boat ride around a small pond. Chris had been in the hospital around two and a half months and they really thought Chris would enjoy getting outside for the fresh air and sunshine. As the nurses and assistants were on the dock helping everyone get out of the paddle boats, Chris saw that one of them wasn't paying a lot of attention. Chris knew the assistant pretty well so he saw a great opportunity to have some fun, and he took it. With his left arm, he gave the guy a little shove trying to knock him off into the pond. Luckily one of the other assistants was able to help him catch his balance before he fell in. Everyone started cracking up with laughter, especially Chris, as he watched everyone else hurry off the dock.

Chris' playfulness and mischievousness was so awesome to see during Chris' hospital stay, and over the years of rehabilitation. I really think his personality helped him through some rough times. '*It's not what you go through in life; it's how you react to your situation*!'

Chapter 32 – Life Events

- June 2011 to May 2019

    Met Laura M, she helped us navigate all of our legal needs including court cases. What a blessing.

- September 30, 2011

    Chris had his first visit with his new PMRD, Dr. Doble, who would oversee Chris' medical life for the next 10 years, and became a friend. (She had also tried to be a matchmaker.)

- September 19, 2011

    Chris met Margie, at Willowbrook, who would oversee his rehabilitation for the next four years. She became an important part of Chris' life, and still is.

- January, 3, 2012

    Chris started eight weeks of hyperbaric treatment for 1.5 hours per day.

- March 13, 2012

    Chris went through artificial bone flap surgery. Helmet retired.

- April 14, 2012

    Chris had been putzing around on his 4-wheeler when the throttle got stuck and sent him flying across the road into a ditch. Thankfully there were no injuries.

- August 10, 2012

    Chris flew to Vanessa and Kyle's destination wedding. He spent four days with family and friends celebrating with the bride and groom.

- September 13, 2012

    At home in his own house, Chris' right foot rolled and he broke a bone in his foot. Six weeks in a walking cast.

- July 29, 2013 to April 2017

    We acquired a case manager on July 29, 2013. Linda L became a very important member of Team Benear for the next four years. She helped us navigate through countless doctor appointments and therapy adventures among other things. Her assistance was invaluable. Wish we had met her years earlier.

- September 24, 2013

    Driving assessment. Had car adjusted for left hand and foot only driving. Chris regained some independence. DRIVING!

- January 29, 2014

  Chris regained his own guardianship.

- June 24, 2014

  Cranioplasty hardware removal for parts that began sticking out of his skull. Chris had surgery to remove two screws and a bracket.

- November 9, 2014

  Chris got his first deer after the accident with his new crossbow. Nephew Jack, 6 years old, and his dad were in the blind with Chris. Big Day.

- 2015

  Doctors seemed to have found the appropriate seizure medication dosages.

- August 2016

  Robert Salmon's brother Todd had a medical condition that placed him on the fourth floor intensive care unit at the U of M hospital. One day Chris and Jeff traveled down the familiar road to spend the afternoon with Todd. To their surprise, Barbara was Todd's nurse that day. When they walked in they were greeted by her with a smile and hugs. Barbara had secretly called Dr. Yang's office to let her know that one of her patients was back. Not telling her who it was, Dr. Yang soon walked in to see that Chris and Jeff were sitting there and again hugs were exchanged. Other nurses Nicole and Becky also stopped in with some other hospital staff that remembered Chris. Todd will tell you that he had plenty of visitors that day, but even though he was the patient, everyone who stopped on that day wanted to see Rambo.

- November 14, 2020

  Chris and I went to say good bye to Aunt Joyce. They were going to start her on morphine through hospice later that evening so we needed to go see her. As we entered Joyce's bedroom, it hit both of us really hard. I quietly talked a lot while we sat with her. Joyce only opened her eyes occasionally. As Chris bent over to give her a kiss on the cheek, she reached up and pulled him down for a hug. It was a long and intense hug with lots of tears. It was one of the most precious moments I had ever witnessed. We said our good byes and heaven gained another angel on 11/18/2020.

Chapter 33 – Family and Friends

Family and friends…the more I look back, they did so much for Jeff, me, and Chris. So much generosity; meals – hugs – treats – socks – puzzle books – journals – mowing – cutting trees – rides – 'Frosty' – prayers – cards – help with my mom – gift cards – listening – checking on houses, and just plain being there with us and for us.

You go through life building up relationships whether you realize you are doing it or not. Attending parties, funerals, graduations, anniversaries, birthdays, bonfires, weddings, card parties, etc. etc. etc. A card sent in the mail or a call just to say hello or spread the word about something or someone also builds relationships. Some relationships take a lot of time and work and others just flow easily no matter how much effort you put into it. Family which is your bloodline or those special people you choose to spend your time with or friendships you have cultivated over time are all blessings.

Shortly after we were notified of Chris' accident those blessings flowed over. We were given so much help and support it was overwhelming. We could spend all of our time concentrating on Chris' needs for his recovery because all of the other little things (everything else seemed little at a time like that) were covered by family and friends.

Food – weeded gardens – found phones – prayers – calls – cut trees – journals – visits – goodies – picked gardens – more mowed lawns – moral support – mowers fixed – gift cards – towed truck – found wallets – hospital stays – fundraisers, all of these acts of kindness meant so much to Team Benear, I hope they all know how thankful and blessed we felt.

There were two outstanding fundraisers that Vanessa and her team hosted. The first was at a Buffalo Wild Wings.

'FIGHTING WITH CHRIS/BUILT TC TOUGH' POSTING – July 14th

Amazing night at Buffalo Wild Wings fundraiser!

The turnout blew us away. We raised over $2000.00 for Chris as we enjoyed wings, drinks, and each other. The wait actually got up to over two hours. Buffalo Wild Wings informed us that it was their BIGGEST fundraiser yet. Vanessa (the organizer) was right.

Everyone went <u>BIG</u> for <u>Chris</u>! Mary (Chris' mom) made a guest appearance and was overwhelmed with love and support. We even celebrated some birthdays (Linda G & Mrs. K) while we were at it too.

Thanks again to everyone (all hundreds of you) that showed your support for Chris and the Benear family. We can't wait for Sunday's event at Cleary's. We hope they are prepared for US.

'FIGHTING WITH CHRIS/BUILT TC TOUGH' POSTING – July 18th

Vanessa and her TEAM did it again at the second fundraiser held at Cleary's in downtown Howell. She had asked Jeff or me to stop by on our way home from the hospital. Jeff was spending the night with Chris so on my way home; I stopped by the fundraiser for a visit. Emotionally, I knew it would be hard, but I was so grateful for all the hard work 'the team' had put into the plans. I knew I needed to stop by to say thanks!!!

When I entered the room where the fundraiser was taking place, I was in total shock. The girls had been talking about all the plans at the hospital at different times when they were there, but I really had no idea how much work they had put into it.

- Everyone seemed to be wearing a 'Built TC Tough' or 'Built CB Tough' shirt.
- There were specialized drink koozies.
- There were rows of tables set up for silent auction donations – food baskets – drink baskets – messages – firewood, cut

and delivered – birdhouses – autographed baseballs – vacation rental in Mexico for a week – restaurant gift cards – Kindle fire basket – autographed sports memorabilia – homemade mirrors – homemade desserts, and on and on.

- There were 50-50 drawings.
- There was food and drink.
- There were CD's of Chris' favorites to hand out.

The list went on and on of special touches the team had thought of. Totally overwhelming. The signs that were posted all over the room, "Fighting with Chris" brought tears to my eyes. I can't believe everything we have been through in the last few weeks and how hard Chris has been fighting for his life. I so wished he could be here to see all the love and support everyone was showing on his behalf.

Our girls were looking at all of the silent auction goodies when they noticed an autographed Nolan Ryan baseball our good family friend Karl P had donated. They called their dad, Jeff, at the hospital and explained to him about a lot of the donations, but that one in particular had caught their eye. Mr. P had said to someone he didn't have a lot of extra money at the time, but he was hoping that the ball would be able to bring in a few bucks. Jeff told Amanda to bid high enough to win that baseball. Karl had already lost his son Danny at the age of twenty-five and for him to think of our son that much it really touched Jeff. The ball was purchased for Jeff. It was in a small glass case on a wooden platform, and was put away in a safe place. Jeff told me his goal was to have Chris give the ball back to Karl when Chris was better.

Seven years later Karl was over for a visit and Jeff thought today would be a good time for the ball to go back to its previous owner. Jeff said to Chris that it was time to give Karl back his baseball and he would like him to do the honors. Chris became a little emotional and told his dad he would rather not. Later that evening Jeff gave Karl a bag to open. "It's not my birthday," Karl had said, "What's this?" Karl opened the bag and realized what it was and grinned from ear to ear. "Never thought I would see this again," he said. Jeff thanked Karl for that special gesture he had made years ago for Chris. They hugged!!!

As I sat and visited with people at different tables the 50-50 drawing was to be up soon. Robert Salmon, Jr. was at my side. He is my twelve year old nephew whose home was where Chris had dragged himself to the night of the accident. I gave him some money to go buy some 50-50 tickets and told him when we win we will split the winnings. Carol M, who was doing a great job as the evening's emcee, was announcing the winning ticket. Robert Jr. came over and said, "Aunt Mary, we WON." I told him to go get the money and donate half of the $210.00 back to the fundraiser, and he could keep $105.00 as his share. He was all smiles as he headed up to collect his winnings. When he told Carol, he would like to donate half back, she made a huge deal out of the generosity of this twelve year old.

He stood there as she told the audience how proud she was of his act of kindness and told everyone if he could do that, they could dig deep in their pockets.

Robert Jr. came back to the table with a sheepish grin as he said, "I forgot to tell her it was your share of the pot I donated." We all laughed.

I was given the microphone, said thank you to a few people, and updated everyone on Chris' condition before I headed out. Not sure exactly what I said, but everyone knew it came from my heart! I cried most of the way home over the amount of support and love I felt in that room. Blessed!!!

So to everyone who supported us, prayed for us, and helped us in any way during this journey that we found ourselves on, Thank you from the bottom of our HEARTS.

Mary

Chapter 34 – Letters to Chris

March 2021

Dear Chris,

This letter was composed in response to your mother's enquiry, and the following statement concerns your impact upon my neurosurgical practice at the University of Michigan. After your acute illness, I have had the pleasure to cross paths with you again on two occasions.

The story begins with a call from a neuro-radiologist to tell me that the patient in the emergency room trauma bay had something inside his brain with the imaging characteristics of "mahogany." Shortly thereafter, the on-call resident neurosurgeon contacted me with the very poor neurological status of the patient. My experience with patients who had significant dominant hemisphere brain trauma with a poor initial neurological examination consisted mostly of young patients who ultimately lost the ability to live independently, often remaining on ventilators with feeding tubes in nursing homes –

so I was already mentally reviewing the "let him go peacefully" speech that I would be having with the patient's family.

My first encounter with your father and mother ensued as I entered the ER. Quite frankly, the raw earnest look in your father's eyes and voice won me over, and I never gave my speech. Instead, I found myself obtaining a consent form for operative intervention, albeit reviewing the loss of independent living as a likely outcome and risk. Then in the operating room soon thereafter with me were a senior resident (now a brain tumor surgeon at a major academic institution on the east coast) and a very junior resident (now a peripheral nerve surgeon at a west coast academic center) – they were in awe as we extracted multiple large pieces of fencepost wood from your brain.

I, however, was in awe of the brain that continued to swell while we ensured that as much of the foreign material was removed as possible.

When we were ready to close, no possibility existed for replacing the piece of skull that we had removed. Consequently, we closed the scalp over the angry brain, and we escorted you to the ICU where I again met with your father and mother.

The ICU course was predictably rocky as you teetered on the edge of brain swelling/herniation for days, portending a poor outcome. However, to the credit of our ICU faculty and your own subconscious intent, you graduated from the ICU to the general care neurosurgery floor, then to our rehabilitation unit. To that point, you had become another young patient with brain trauma who had significant neurological deficits.

Weeks afterward, I did my rounds on you in the rehabilitation unit to look at your scalp wound, but with your eyes and your non-paralyzed arm, you gestured for me to stay. In fact, you were moving cards one-handed as therapy. At a cursory glance, I was sure that you were not actually playing cards. But after I played a round with you, I realized that you were, in fact, playing cards and recovering cognitively very well – because you beat me.

Your outpatient follow-up was similarly memorable because I sustained a bruise on my arm during one of your follow-up visits. Since we had yet to replace the piece of skull that we had removed, you visited me in the outpatient clinic multiple times. On one occasion, I entered the clinic room and enthusiastically greeted you with "Hi, Woody!" (In fact, my administrative assistant from those years happened to walk by my office just now as the photo of the intraoperative wood pieces is on my computer screen, and she says, "There's Woody!" I am sure that you can figure out how you earned that nickname.) Before I enunciated the "y" in Woody, our nurse practitioner hit my arm so hard as to make me stumble sideways, whispering loudly, "That's Chris; that's Chris."...... not Woody. And so the skull flap was replaced, and I understood that you regained the ability to live in your own home.

Since then, I have followed you from afar; once, the ICU nurses called me because you were in house visiting a friend with an aneurysmal rupture, and later from a photograph of you with your family and friends. Each time, I remember that you are the person who reminds me that despite mortal circumstances, everyone deserves a chance at life.

Best regards,

Lynda
Lynda Yang, M.D., Ph.D.

January 2021

Dear Bean –

I cannot believe that I am able to write you a letter and actually still give it to you. Nearly 10 years ago, you survived an accident that was unsurvivable!

My family became friends with your family back in the clogging days. Amanda and I would tear up that dance floor as young kids! Over the years, we continued to grow close; we created some unforgettable memories, and a profound friendship, one that I cherish every day and forever!

I'll never forget the day that I learned of your accident. We had just spent an early summer day enjoying the weather and water on Lake Chemung with friends. You didn't make it home that night. Instead, you endured one of the most life changing events in your life. Somehow, you crawled out of a ravine that your truck had soared into.

We don't know how, but you survived and can now share an incredible story of perseverance, and determination. We visited you in the hospital for months, prayed for you, journaled, celebrated you with fundraisers, and helped you fight for recovery and the precious life that you are now able to live!

Two years later, you were able to travel to Mexico for Kiel's and my wedding. We were so grateful that you were able to make it. Sawyer is five now and is proud to call you Uncle Bean!

You have always been independent and determined! I wish we could all have your strength and courage. Whether you know it or not, you amaze me every day! Thanks for being an inspiration and an amazing friend! Life wouldn't be the same without you! Love you Bean!

Love always –Vanessa L

January 2021

Chris,

At times it seems like we were at the hospital an eternity ago, but then there are moments where it seems like only yesterday. Your ability to adapt and endure amazes me, and I hope you know how inspiring you are to me and everyone who has heard the story of your accident, survival, and recovery.

I am not even sure where to begin or how to find the words to express my feelings about you and your perseverance over the last 10 years. I remember being at the hospital the morning after your accident, seeing you, and hearing the conversations and concerns about how severe your injuries were. The concerns regarding your recovery and how you were going to make it through the next few days were unnerving; the medical staff had not seen injuries of that severity and just didn't know what the first few days would be like. In all fairness to the doctors and nurses, they were only relying on their medical experiences and had no clue how strong willed, determined, and relentless your resolve was and still is. It was still heart-wrenching and scary to see the extent of your injuries. The unknown was frightening. We all leaned on each other, praying for your survival and using the knowledge of your will to fight as our foundation to stay strong for you and for each other.

Your hunger for winning and not accepting anything less can be seen daily in your drive to continue your recovery, continue getting stronger, and continuing to find ways to enjoy the things that you love. I remember being in the pumpkin patch last year spraying the weeds, and you were running your backpack sprayer, then we switched and I took a turn running the sprayer. I just kept thinking how does Chris make running this sprayer look so easy, and then I remembered, this is TC we are talking about, defeat is not an option.

I know things are not always easy and I only hope you know that we are all here to continue to support you and your recovery, and we are so thankful that you made the choice to climb out of that ravine and fight to stay here with us. Always keep fighting and always remember you are built "TC" tough. Love you!

Liz

January 2021

Kissyfur,

Thank you so much for being you. You didn't give up on the night of your accident and to this day you keep fighting to improve and to keep living the best life you can live. Day after day, the doctors would tell us to prepare to say goodbye, but they didn't know you like we knew you. We knew you were nowhere near quitting. We knew that you had come too far to give up and that our prayers and GMA's prayers joining you in your fight would conquer any risk of further infection. We knew with your dedication and our strength in numbers, the doctors wouldn't be able to stop you from achieving more than they had ever imagined. From the 100+ sleepless nights in the hospital to countless therapy sessions once you were home, and to this day, we are thankful for you and thankful you've never stopped fighting.

Through everything that has happened over the last ten years, the one thing we will forever be thankful for is you. You still being you, and you always being present. My favorite quote from Bryn to date is, "I love Uncle Bean because he talks to me." The only Uncle Bean Bryn knows and loves is the same man that I've known and loved my whole life. He's the Uncle Bean who takes the time to talk with her, includes her in every adventure, and is always there for us. From visits to see your pigs and gator rides around the neighborhood to help with the pumpkins and every other aspect of the farm. It doesn't feel like much to you, but it means the world to her and me. We look forward to every visit and every hug.

We love you. Our family wouldn't be the same without you. The farm wouldn't be the same without you. We wouldn't be the same without you.

Love,

Emmers

January 2021

Dear Chris,

On June 3, 2011, you were tasked with helping set up the party tent at the B's for Steph's bridal shower. I rode with you, not really to help (of course not) but "supervise." You were doing all of the work. After the tent was up, we shared a couple of beers with friends and headed home. On the way back to mom and dad's house, we chatted non-stop. We talked about my kids. We talked about sports. We talked about Howell gossip; even though that was something you were never interested in. Then we stopped at Wendy's and you only ordered one burger. We laughed, reminiscing about your high school days and how one burger was merely a "snack" before the real meal. In that moment, I was intensely proud of you.

I left for college before you were a "man", only 16 at the time. But there you were now 13 years later. I was in awe of the man you had become. You were a smart man, a great friend, a loyal brother, and a wonderful uncle. You were TC. You were the brother who was never afraid to give me shit when he disagreed with me, which was almost always. You were the brother who always hugged me so hard it physically hurt. Little did I know that just a few short days later, your world (and ours) would change. The moments, days, and months that followed are a blur. I know they were for you too.

The emotions were painful. The fear was immense. I did not know whether I would be able to talk to you again, to tell you I love you. I did not know if you would ever be able to hug me again. I did not know if you would be able to watch my kids grow and teach them all of the things you know so well. After all, there is only one Uncle Bean—only one like you.

I watched mom and dad crumble. Over, and over, and over. And yet, despite their constant emotional pain, they were there for you, every single second. The love they have for you is all-encompassing. Their hope for your recovery was the constant that kept us all praying.

Every day you gave us another miracle. Each time we were told to fear the worst, you gave us the best. Each time. You overcame all obstacles. I will never forget the moment after your plate surgery when Dr. Yang hugged dad. Dad and Dr. Yang did not have the best relationship. Dr. Yang had given dad your diagnosis, and dad rejected it. "Not Chris," he would say, "Chris is stronger than any other patient you know." You proved dad right. Dr. Yang held dad and told him that you were a medical miracle. She said that you changed the way she practices medicine. She said that you defied science. There is no explanation for that, except you, and the extraordinary person you are.

I don't know how any one individual is brave enough, strong enough, and dedicated enough to endure what you did. I don't know what inspired you that evening to live. I don't know how you withstood the pain. I don't know how you continued to fight when the darkness was so immense. I don't know what thoughts or hopes you held on to, when you continued to climb, drag, and haul your physically shattered body to get help. I don't know how you defied every medical opinion. I don't know how you proved science wrong. I simply don't know.

What I do know, is you. You are brave. You are strong. You are smart. You are resourceful. You are resilient. You are a fighter. You are a warrior. You are an inspiration. You are a miracle. You are TC. I am flooded with gratitude for your will to fight. I am thankful that my children still get to play with and learn from you. I am happy (kind of) that your hugs are still so strong that they cause me physical pain. I am insanely proud of the man you are today.

I love you, brother.

Amanda

January 2021

Brother,

I've called you my best friend for longer than I can remember. When I think back on my childhood and all the great times I've had, you are a part of them all. You and I have always had a close relationship and I wouldn't change it for anything. I always say we are like twins, just born 17 months apart. Heck, even our annoying thin hair is the same! My favorite memories with you include going out every weekend and dancing the night away at Snappers, racing you to Oak Grove and back while you kicked my butt even though you hadn't run in years (I was training daily for college ball), and singing 'The Dance' every time there was a karaoke night and asking me after, "How did I do? No for real, was I good?" Thanks for being such a great friend growing up, I couldn't have asked for a better brother to hang out with.

You've always been tough, a little cocky, but tough. ☺ All your constant injuries growing up through football and motorcycle accidents never seemed to set you back, but rather pushed you harder. Guess God was preparing you…toughening you up! But boy did he! And man I am so thankful he did. Brother, you are honestly the toughest person I know…can't believe I just said that out loud. I'm going to be hearing about it for the rest of our lives, ☺ but you are!

One of the hardest things I've ever done is to go through one of the happiest days of my life without you there. Even writing that, I realize that my hard days don't even compare to your hard days. I'm sorry you were not able to be at my wedding. I'm sorry that you couldn't play football anymore because of all your injuries. I'm sorry you were so close to realizing your dream of becoming an electrician, and that it didn't happen. I'm sorry that you had your old life ripped away from you without notice. I'm sorry that you have had to relearn everything (although I'm not sure you ever lost your ability to give people shit). But, I'm not sorry that you are here. I know this life is not what you had planned or how you thought it would be, but I admire your grit, determination, and positive outlook on what you can control! You inspire me every day and I look up to you more than you'll ever know!

Thank you for still putting me in my place when I need it. Thank you for working so hard in therapy. Thank you for fighting that night. Thank you for the way you are with my kids, they adore their Uncle Bean. You single handedly make their day with your loud, grand entrances. And only you can hassle my kids and give them the 'claw' and yet they still keep coming back for more. I will forever be grateful for the relationship you have built with my kids; you are such a huge part of their lives. Thank you. ☺

Also, you have changed my life. Your fight to get yourself help, your perseverance through countless hours of therapies, and your positive outlook in the hardest of times has completely changed my perspective and goals. You have made me appreciate the small things; feeding pigs, spaghetti dinners, playing Uno, and gator sledding!

But of all the GREAT things you have done in your life…being named Melon Prince, scoring countless touchdowns, taking down the biggest bucks, and even running your own business…watching you fight to get where you are today makes me so proud. I am proud to call you, not just my brother, but my forever buddy for life. Thank you for fighting…you will never know how much that has meant to me and every single person whose life you are a part of. Thank you for being you! Thank you for the dance! ☺

It only feels right to end with you and me singing 'The Dance' together…

Stephanie

January 2021

Christopher John,

I would like to start out by just saying thank you because on June 5, 2011 you made a choice, not just for you, but for all of us – your family and friends. It was your will to survive, courage, and determination that kept you alive long enough for someone to help. Once you were at the hospital, for you your life was in the balance, for me it was the worst nightmare I could ever imagine. The first news we had was that your chance of survival was not good. My inner soul could not accept that. This is my son and my son is not your average cat. When he decides he is going to do something it happens, and this situation is no different. Hearing the news, I walked over to where you lay on the gurney in the emergency department and I said, "Chris, I know you can hear me, you need to pull out all the stops and run the <u>Money</u> <u>Play</u>." (Remember that offensive play in football that was designed for you, and when nothing else worked and the team was backed up the Money Play would always work?)

It's been almost 10 years since that day and I have to say I am so PROUD of you and your effort, spending countless hours in various rehab programs trying to get your life back. In my opinion you have done an awesome job. If you stop and think about where you started and how you are now, you're absolutely <u>incredible</u>. Even today you are still trying to get stronger gain back the balance and agility you had before your injury. You are definitely a person who never gives up. Like I said almost 10 years ago, you're not the average cat, you're my son.

"Half Man, Half Amazing."

I will always be there for you no matter what.

Love,

Dad

January 2021

Dear Son,

Ten years – I can't believe it's been that long since we learned of your accident. From the minute the police knocked on our door to tell us the bad news, all I could think about was getting to you as fast as I could. I prayed so hard for God to be with you. When I walked into the emergency department, I had never felt so much pain in seeing my little boy lying there and there was nothing I could do. I felt helpless. When I found out what you had to go through on your path of survival after your truck veered off the road, my heart ached.

I am so proud of the man you are. I know you have touched a lot of lives by the outpouring of love and support we were shown during your ordeal. I know during your journey of life you have been dealt some hard obstacles, but you constantly keep fighting to overcome those obstacles to succeed in improving your life.

Thank you –

- For being such a survivor and fighter,
- for being a role model on what will and determination can accomplish,
- for the hugs,
- for giving your dad good hunting tips and for being his best friend,

- for making me smile inside every time you smile and say "Are you ready?" even though I know the likelihood of me winning a game is pretty slim,
- for being patient (most of the time) when you have to repeat things to be understood,
- for making my world so special by just being YOU!!!

Love,

Mom

P.S. I hope you get your hunting <u>land</u>!

Chapter 35 – Chris' Journey Continues

January 2021

My son's accident was ten years ago (as of June 5, 2021), but for Jeff and me, at times, it seems like it was yesterday. We can both tear up at the mention of a story that has anything to do with Chris' accident or his recovery process. I'll admit my tears have flowed a lot over the last few years.

Hard working, strong, loving, stubborn, independent, diligent, caring, focused, and humorous all described Chris pre-accident. Now we can add courageous, brave, determined, adaptable, feisty, persevering, and strong willed to that list. Through Chris' efforts to save his life, he showed us all what he is made of.

Chris is still an avid hunter, using a crossbow has yielded some nice bucks. One of his favorite pastimes is still playing cards. It is really hard to beat him in card games of skill. Mom does better on games of chance. Chris goes to the gym three times a week with one day being spent in the pool. He loves working with his tractor on moving brush or grading his drive and road. He has a special bond with nieces and nephews and loves being around them, but after a while Chris will disappear in his gator and head home for some peace and quiet. Chris has never recovered the functional use of his right hand, but he has learned to adapt to a lot of different circumstances.

The bond of family and friends is still strong and very supportive. We are trying to pay all the blessings we received forward, but it will take a while. Team Benear will always remember everyone who played any part in helping us all, especially Chris, to get through this period in our lives.

The best the doctors can surmise is that Chris had a heat stroke that changed our lives forever which made us appreciate and be thankful for the journey we have had, and the journey yet to come.

Family and Friends

Christopher (Chris) Benear – son of Jeff and Mary Benear

Jeff Benear – Chris' father

Mary Benear – Chris' mother (author)

Amanda B F – Chris' oldest sister

Justin F – Amanda's husband/Chris' brother-in-law

Jack F – Amanda and Justin's son/Chris' nephew

Stephanie B – Chris' older sister

Alex R – Stephanie B's fiancé/husband

Ali K – family friend

Allen S – Jeff's brother/Chris' Uncle

Amelia B – Chris' cousin

Andrew – Chris' nephew

Bain – Chris' friend

Mama Bain – Chris' friend's mother

Barbara – Chris' nurse

Ben N – Chris' friend

Betty B – Mary's sister/Chris' Aunt

Carol S – Mary's sister/Chris' Aunt

Cheryl O'H – family friend

Cynda B – family friend

Dana Michelle – Chris' cousin

Dave B – Betty's husband/Chris' Uncle

Emily B – Chris' cousin

'Fifty' – Chris' friend

Howard – Chris' cousin

Jake F – Chris' softball buddy

Jamie F – cousin

Jeff and Sue P – family friends

Jen A – family friend

Jen G – family friend

Jenn A – family friend

Jessica B – family friend

Jodi F – Chris' cousin

John B – good family friend, nicknamed Uncle Buffalo

Judy S – Allen S's wife/Chris' Aunt

Karl P – good family friend

Kiel C – Chris' friend

Kristi W – Chris' friend

Laura – family friend

Liz B – Chris' cousin

Linda B – Chris' honorary Aunt

Linda B – good family friend

Linda L – case worker extraordinaire

Linda M B – good family friend

Mark C – Chris' friend

Marv – Chris' friend

Nancy B – Mary's sister/Chris' Aunt

Nate F – Chris' good friend

Norm K – Jeff's sister's husband/Chris' Uncle

Paula K – Jeff's sister/Chris' Aunt

Phil W – Chris' uncle

Robert S – Carol's husband/Chris' Uncle

Ron M – Neighbor and friend

Ronda B – Chris' Aunt, John's wife

Ryan M – Chris' friend

Sarah P – family friend

Sarah V – Chris' good friend

Sharon & Don – Chris' Aunt and her husband

Stacy – Chris' cousin

Stephanie W – Chris' nurse

Steve B – Nancy's husband/Chris' Uncle

Tigger – family friend

Todd S – Robert S's brother

Vanessa (Nessie) – good family friend

Acknowledgments

Thank you to Janet Weber for all of her extensive help and patience with the editing of this book. The calls, meetings, questions, ideas, laughs, and tears we have shared these last two years have been so comforting to me on this journey. You have been such a good friend as you helped me maneuver through the writing of this book.

Thanks to Dave Dilworth for your 'dos and don'ts' from your book experience and for sharing it with me. Also, thank you for wanting me to succeed.

Thanks to Team Benear (family and friends) for being the most supportive TEAM I've had the pleasure of working with. You were all there 10 years ago and continue to give unwavering support.

Thank you to Carol and Robert for calling for help and to Dave and Betty for showing up to the hospital within minutes of us, and helping us through those excruciating early hours.

Thanks to Amanda, Justin, Stephanie, and Alex for all you did and are doing to support your brother, Chris. We know when dad and I are gone, Chris is in good hands and we are at peace knowing that.

Thank you to my husband Jeff for his encouragement and confidence that I would succeed at putting Chris' story to print. For forty two years of loving me for who I am.

Thanks to Chris. There is nothing more I can say except thanks for being you!!